It Happened In Se

It Happened In Michigan

Remarkable Events That Shaped History

Colleen Burcar

gpp

Guilford, Connecticut

Map by Daniel Lloyd © Morris Book Publishing, LLC

Library of Congress Cataloging-in-Publication Data is available on file.

ISBN 978-0-7627-6024-4

Printed in the United States of America

10 9 8 7 6 5 4

CONTENTS

MICHIGAN

CONTENTS

INTRODUCTION

Without question, Michigan is one of a kind. Admitted into the Union as the twenty-sixth state on January 26, 1837, Michigan is the only two-part state, with the dual peninsulas now happily bridged together by the Mighty Mac. During their space travels, astronauts have reportedly been able to easily identify Michigan as it stands out clearly outlined by the magnificence of the Great Lakes: No matter where you are in the state, you're never more than eighty-six miles from either Lakes Huron, Ontario, Michigan, Erie, or Superior. Covering more than 31,700 square miles, Lake Superior alone contains ten percent of all the fresh water on the planet. Bodies of water cover about 41 percent of this "blue water" state, making it truly a water wonderland.

We can give partial credit for our beauty to our neighbor, for it was the Wisconsin Glacier that gave Michigan its distinctive geographic characteristics. The uniquely spirited sand dunes began as glacial debris. The strong Lake Michigan winds continue to move the dunes forward, as much as three feet each year. Rich diversity exists in other natural resources: enormous salt fields; the once-prosperous mines, housing iron ore and copper; landscapes of mountainous forests; and pristine cliffs. Fertile soil gives birth to top-producing food crops, including sugar beets, cherries, potatoes, apples, and beans.

Throughout the years, the state has been host to a medley of cultures, which have not always coexisted peacefully. From the early struggles among the American Indians, the French, and the British, to the modern-day clashes between the races, to the numerous labor disputes, Michigan has conquered its brushes with adversity to reunite stronger than ever.

Michiganders, Michiganians, or whatever you choose to call us, are proud, resilient people. History has proven that. I, too, am honored to be classified as a lifer, someone who has spent her entire life here, yet, admittedly, I still have so much to learn about our historical wealth.

The following thirty stories are designed to expand our knowledge of events that have helped shape Michigan. For me, their discovery was similar to a treasure hunt: I knew I was searching for something, yet I was uncertain what I would actually find. Open-ended research afforded me endless possibilities, each more interesting than the next. After combing through pages and pages of material, I'd land on a gem that would instantly inspire me to say, "I never knew that."

Michigan has perhaps had more than its share of tragedies. Surprisingly, one of them struck a very personal chord with me. While combing through the names of victims from the 1913 Italian Hall catastrophe in Calumet, I came across Victoria Burcar, age nine years, four months, of Croatian descent. I learned that she was one of my relatives, who had faced a tragic, untimely death. An instant connection was formed to someone I never knew existed.

There were happy revelations, too, through some of our amazing sports teams, including the little-known high school team from Saginaw's Arthur Hill that accomplished a feat that may never be repeated anywhere in America.

The stories in this book are meant to awaken and stimulate our appreciation of the fascinating events that are part of Michigan's genealogy.

I thank all my friends who constantly fed me ideas. A special thank-you to Dave Lochner, who fattened my mind with so many tidbits that his goal was to be listed as coauthor. I am grateful to all the librarians at the Bloomfield Township Public Library who spent countless hours retrieving materials from their archives. Also deserving of appreciation are two exceptional people from St. Joseph: Alicia Allen from the St. Joseph Public Library and Chris Hartman from the Berrien County Clerk's Office. Both of them were wonderful and went out of their way to dig up numerous hard-to-find facts for me.

And last, but not least, a special expression of thanks and love to my husband, Bryan Becker, for putting up with me during this arduous investigative project. His red editing pen put in umpteen hours of overtime, all while watching his beloved Detroit Tigers.

PAGEANT OF THE SAULT

1671

The dramatic spectacle, a year in the making, was almost under way. The participants were lined up, costumed in European finery. Members of the audience had traveled far, some of them for months, to witness this historical event that would change the way the rest of the world would look at Michigan for the next hundred years.

Chippewa Indians were the first known inhabitants of this eastern end of the Upper Peninsula, setting up their tepees along the banks of the flowing rapids. By 1668 they had new neighbors: Father Jacques Marquette, a French Jesuit priest, accompanied by another priest and a lay brother. Establishing the first mission in the region with permanent structures, Marquette appropriately named the area Sault Ste. Marie, after Saint Mary, the Blessed Virgin Mother *Sault* in French is loosely translated as "rapids." Putting the words together, Sault Ste. Marie means the Rapids of St. Mary.

The Sault came abundantly blessed with wildlife. The Indians appreciated the wealth of nourishment they found in the rushing waters. In fact, the whitefish were so plentiful that the missionaries claimed they "could easily catch enough to feed 10,000 men."

The French, hoping to enlarge their empire, had been monitoring the Indians from afar and soon realized the time was ripe to stake their claim on the territory here. During the summer of 1670, Jean Talon, Intendant of Justice, Police, and Finance, began to set the stage in Michigan for France's ambitions: to expand New France's colonies throughout North America. And along with colonial expansion came the enormous profits from the burgeoning fur trade.

It was determined that the "takeover" would be conducted in the form of an elaborate pageant. The role of director and mastermind was assigned to Simon François Daumont, Sieur de St. Lusson, a French soldier of fortune. Assistance would be needed to connect with the Native Americans. So the role of "actors" was given to Nicolas Perrot, who for five years had lived with various tribes in Wisconsin, and explorer Louis Jolliet.

The command was given to recruit tribes from a distance of a hundred leagues (roughly four to five hundred miles) or more. Gathering an audience from faraway places would take time. A full twelve months beforehand, Perrot ventured back to Green Bay, where he met with chiefs of the Menominee, Winnebago, Potawatami, and Sauk tribes. He convinced them to migrate to Sault Ste. Marie for this once-in-a-lifetime theatrical presentation on behalf of the king of France. Likewise, Jolliet summoned other tribes.

The following year, with some 2,000 Indians representing fourteen different tribes assembled and all participants in place, the Pageant of the Sault was set to begin on June 14, 1671. After a typically long and blustery winter, Mother Nature had now provided the most picturesque staging possible, according to early Jesuit writings, "beside the foaming waters of the straits, with dark pines and hemlocks standing attentive."

Leading the solemn procession was St. Lusson, radiantly adorned in a stately uniform of a seventeenth-century French officer. Following him were Jesuit priests and various other French officials, all properly attired. A large wooden cross was ceremoniously planted in the ground and then blessed, followed by the singing of the sixth-century hymn "Vexilla Regis Prodeunt." Those present could immediately feel an infectious joy, perhaps a sign of hope for the Indians. The French escutcheon was then placed above the cross while the Exaudiat, the twentieth Psalm, was sung.

The crowning moment of this spectacle came when St. Lusson, declaring himself an official representative of the king, lifted his sword and proclaimed three times that all lands discovered or yet to be discovered in North America now belonged to the "Most High, Most Mighty and Most Redoubtable Monarch Louis the XIV of the Name, Most Christian King of France and Navarre." Official papers were presented and then signed by all the white men in attendance. Muskets were shot off as the Indians cheered wildly, even though they hadn't understood a single word of what had been spoken. Everyone in the crowd was filled with excitement.

After the assemblage quieted, Father Claude Allouez, serving as a translator, attempted to explain to the Indians what they had just witnessed. His objective was to offer such praise of the king that they would be left awestruck. Allouez spoke slowly and with determination, addressing the questioning eyes of his audience. In an official state paper, published by Pierre Margry, author unknown, it is stated that he first declared Jesus Christ as the "master of our lives, of Heaven, of Earth, and of Hell," followed by encouragement to observe the French crest placed above the cross. Referring to the earthly king, his descriptions were eloquently verbose:

He is the captain of the greatest captains, and has not his equal in the world. All the captains you have ever seen, or of whom you have ever heard, are mere children compared with him. He is like a great tree, and they, only like little plants that we tread under foot in walking. . . . Your canoes hold only four or five men, or, at the very most, ten or twelve. Our ships in France hold four or five hundred, and even as many as a thousand. . . . Other men make war by land, but in such vast number, that if drawn up in double file they would reach from here to Mackinac. When he attacks he is more terrible than the thunder: the earth trembles, the air and sea are set on fire by the discharges of his cannon; while he has been seen amid his quadroons all covered with the blood of his foes, of whom he has slain so many with his sword that he does not count their scalps, but the rivers of blood which he sets flowing. . . . From all parts of the world people go to listen to his words and to admire him, and he alone decides all the affairs of the world. . . . What shall I say of his wealth? You count yourselves rich when you have ten or twelve sacks of corn, some hatchets, glass beads, kettles or other things of that sort. He has towns of his own, more in number than you have people in all these countries five hundred leagues around. . . . His house is longer than from here to the head of the Sault, that is, more than half a league and higher than the tallest of your trees.

Allouez continued with his effusive praise of King Louis, leaving the Indians flabbergasted.

The ritual concluded with a waterside bonfire and a hymn of thanksgiving for all those "poor peoples, that they were now the subjects of so great and powerful a monarch."

The king now owned them all. It was through this pageant that France annexed every bit of the interior lands of North America, leaving the British even more confused than the Indians.

THE *GRIFFON* SETS SAIL

1679

The burgeoning fur-trading business in northern Michigan was the impetus behind French explorer René-Robert Cavelier, Sieur de La Salle's desire to create the first seafaring vessel on the Great Lakes. In 1679 water travel was limited to the Native Americans' birch-bark canoes. Just twelve to forty feet long, the canoes were slow-moving and could negotiate the current only near the shoreline. But La Salle was seeking a quicker method of transportation that would enable him to sell large quantities of his furs to faraway places like China and Japan.

Loyal to his homeland, the highly ambitious La Salle, one of only twenty-five licensed fur traders in the area, also longed to expand France's empire around the world. Money was not easy to come by, and he was already operating his business at a loss. At his settlement in St. Ignace, he pondered every conceivable way he could make his dreams come true.

Then his entrepreneurial creativeness kicked in. He would build his own ship, cutting down on expensive freight charges and easing his dependence on outside travel sources. He wondered why he hadn't thought of this brilliant idea earlier.

Putting his plan into action wasn't without obstacles. First, there was the issue of money. At the moment, he had none and was forced to find a lender willing to take the risk, offering the astronomical interest rate of 40 percent. Next, he needed a rather large building site, but the Indians were highly possessive of their territory. They were also quite suspicious and fearful of the "big canoe" that was being proposed. After exploring numerous sites, La Salle realized that his best option would be to construct his envisioned boat in the wilderness on the Niagara River.

Carpenters worked all winter long, using local white pine to bring to life the seventy-foot, forty-five-ton vessel that would become the first ship ever to sail the Great Lakes. The ship was christened the *Griffon,* and an emblem of a griffin—the mythological creature that was half eagle, half lion—was meticulously carved on both the bow and the stern.

With its seven brass cannons mounted on the sides, no one was quite sure whether it was a commercial craft or a warship. Whatever it was, La Salle was ecstatic. His good friend and confidant, Father Louis Hennepin, kept a detailed journal throughout the construction, noting that as the Indians watched it being built, they "expressed some discontent at what we were doing." Further on he wrote that the builders "made all the haste we could to get it afloat . . . to prevent the designs of the natives who had resolved to burn it." The ship had a likability problem right from the start.

When the *Griffon* was finally ready for its inaugural launch, La Salle reportedly cried out in a loud voice, "High above the black crows shall the gallant griffon soar." Soar she did on her first trip, on August 6, with a motley crew of thirty-four, including the proud new owner.

At the ship's helm was an odd sort of character. Standing seven feet tall, Luke the Dane was known for his violent temper and an attitude that spoke, "Does not work well with others." Yet he was a good pilot and was needed if the *Griffon* was to be a success. But he, like the other members of the crew, had not been paid in over a year, causing additional irritability.

Despite a few bouts of nasty weather, the maiden voyage went smoothly, transporting furs across Lake Erie to Detroit, through Fort Michilimackinac on the way to Green Bay. Along the way, they crossed into a small body of water on August 12, the feast day of Saint Clair of Assisi. Paying homage to his Catholic faith, La Salle declared that this new waterway would forever be known as "Lake St. Clair."

With one profitable round-trip journey behind her, it was time to prove her real value. It was a trip that would be remembered for centuries. On September 18, the *Griffon* and its crew of six, including Luke, loaded 12,000 pounds of beaver pelts on board in preparation for the trip back to Green Bay. Hennepin penned his observations as the ship sailed away as well as rumors of what he heard days later: "They sailed . . . with a westerly wind. The ship came to an anchor to the north of Lake Michigan where she was seen by some Savages, who told us that they advised our men to sail along the coast and not towards the middle of the lake, because of the sands that make the navigation dangerous when there is any high wind. Our pilot, Luke . . . was dissatisfied and would steer where he pleased. . . . The ship was hardly a league from the coast when it was tossed up by a violent storm in such a manner that our men were never heard of since."

That was it. The once-celebrated vessel was gone, as if it had vanished into thin air. The *Griffon,* including her crew and cargo, was never to be seen or heard from again, resulting in the greatest unsolved mystery of the Great Lakes. Unlike other shipwrecks in the record books, which have definable explanations such as "stranded," "capsized," or "ran aground," the *Griffon* has only one word after it: "disappeared."

As expected, La Salle was heartsick and immediately began theorizing about what had happened. The most logical explanation was that the ship simply got caught up in a huge storm. But there were other possibilities: It broke apart, and the Indians captured any survivors. Or it was burned beyond recognition. Or it was destroyed after Luke sold all the furs and kept the money for himself.

No one knows, and likely no one will ever know. No one has found any sign of its wreckage under the sea, although for centuries divers have tried relentlessly to solve this puzzle. If anyone ever discovers the *Griffon*, it will be akin to finding the Holy Grail.

CHIEF PONTIAC'S SIEGE
ON FORT DETROIT

1763

His physical strength was greater than that of any man his age. Sharp-edged bones were used to pierce his nose and ears, and tattoos covered much of his body. The skin on his face was soft and smooth, from both lack of a beard and his daily moisturizing with bear fat. Those who knew him well described him as "proud, vindictive, war-like and an easily offended man." Today he would be known as the general in charge of combat. In 1763 he was known as Pontiac, the great Ottawa Indian chief, determined to expel the British from his territory.

At Fort Detroit, the French and the Native Americans lived side by side in harmony. By providing the French with the materials for a good fur coat or hat, the Indians maintained friendly relations with the French. With their exceptional hunting skills and access to sacred tribal grounds housing the near-extinct yet popular beaver, the Ottawas were able to fulfill their neighbors' desire for what became known as "brown gold." Records show that in one year a single trading company shipped enough beaver pelts overseas to make more than half a million hats. In return, the Europeans outfitted the Indians with guns, enhancing the Indians' ability to hunt and defend themselves and enabling them to transition away from bows and arrows.

Overall, it appeared to be a win-win situation for the two distinctly different cultures—that is, until the British arrived on the scene. After several years of defeating the French elsewhere, the British made their move into Detroit in November 1760. Under the direction of the highly successful and powerful commander-in-chief Sir Jeffrey Amherst, troops entered the settlement with two objectives: to conquer the French on this site and to get rid of what they deemed were the useless Native Americans.

First things first. The British began squeezing the French from various encampments in North America, primarily in Canada, around Quebec and Montreal. The British were applying pressure from all sides, and their oppressive cannons were just too much for the French. The French governor of Canada capitulated to the British, and although no direct combat took place in Detroit, it was officially ceded on November 28, 1760.

With the French now out of power, the British held meetings with the Indians. But during their discussions they withheld the real crux of the matter: that all residents of the area were now subjects of the Crown, no matter what their race or ethnicity.

Major Robert Rogers was in charge of the transition of possession, and fittingly, he had to confront the man in charge of those he was now possessing. He described his introductory meeting with Chief Pontiac in his journal:

> *Ponteack is their present King or Emperor. . . . He puts on an air of majesty and princely grandeur and*

is greatly revered by his subjects. . . . He assured me,
that he was inclined to live peaceably with the English
while they used him as he deserved . . . but intimated,
that, if they treated him with neglect, he should shut up
the way, and exclude them from it.

The warning had been given: Pontiac was not going to stand by quietly and witness his people being mistreated.

The British were unable to grasp what was needed to keep the Ottawa tribe happy. Unlike the French, the British immediately stopped supplying the Ottawas with guns, began rationing food, and required all trading to take place at faraway designated trading posts.

Word of Pontiac's discontent with the British, partially prompted by his dream of the Great Spirit telling him to "wipe them from the face of the earth," spread throughout what was to become Ohio and the rest of the Great Lakes region. Support came from many different tribes, including the Potawatamis, Senecas, Hurons, and Ojibwas, from as far as upstate New York.

Close to five hundred warriors gathered on April 27, 1763, on the banks of the Ecorse River, roughly ten miles from Detroit, to hear their new leader and master orator lay out his plans for attack, scheduled for the following week.

On Sunday, May 1, Pontiac, along with fifty chosen warriors, conned his way into the fort, announcing that they had come to perform a ceremonial dance. With all the boisterous moves and whooping and hollering of the dancers, no one noticed the ten warriors who slipped away silently to canvass the fort's layout. Afterward, Pontiac and the warriors politely left, offering to return with a larger crew for an even more spectacular display of their talents.

Three hundred did return. Only this time, under their garments they had hidden knives, sawed-off muskets, and tomahawks. Yet once inside, Pontiac, keenly perceptive, sensed that something was wrong. It became apparent to him that the British had been alerted to his plan. Subsequently, the attack was called off.

Who could have turned on the Indians and leaked news of the impending onslaught? Legend has it that a young Potawatami woman had fallen in love with the fort's Major Gladwin, and rather than lose him at the hands of Pontiac, she became the scheming informant. Eventually, in a drunken stupor, she lost her own life by falling into a vat of boiling maple syrup.

To save face among the tribes, Pontiac declared all-out war on the British. In the next few days, nearly a dozen whites were killed and scalped. For hours, the Indian warriors fired muskets at the fort.

Yet far more successful attacks were occurring in outlying regions. Tribes had easily conquered Fort Sandusky, Fort St. Joseph in Niles, Fort Miami in Ohio, and Fort LeBoeuf in Waterford, Pennsylvania. The Indians had fired on thirteen forts and were victorious in nine of these attacks.

The British became so agitated (and humiliated) that they knew they had to strike back. Again, because of Pontiac's astuteness, he was fully prepared for the British attack on July 31. The moon was full that night, an advantage for the Indians. At 2:30 a.m., as the British were heard stomping over a wooden bridge, Pontiac's warriors ambushed them, killing twenty and wounding thirty-nine. As the bodies fell into Parent's Creek, they bled so profusely that the water literally turned bright red. Hence, the encounter became forever known as the Battle of Bloody Run.

The attempt to triumph over Fort Detroit appeared to go on forever, and Pontiac's warriors were fast becoming disenchanted. He finally issued a letter of surrender to none other than Major Gladwin on October 31, 1763, giving up the Indians' fight to take the fort. The dominance of the once-great warrior chief had waned considerably, forcing him to find exile in Illinois. His earthly journey ended on April 20, 1769, when he was assassinated by a Peoria Indian.

Pontiac's burial site has been a source of great speculation. Some think his body was brought across the Mississippi River and laid to rest in Missouri. But others believe that Pontiac's final resting place is back home in Michigan, in the very center of Orchard Lake, on the serenely secluded Apple Island.

BATTLE OF THE RIVER RAISIN

1813

The notion of Kentucky and Michigan militiamen fighting side by side for a common cause might be difficult to imagine. But in 1813, that's precisely what happened, as the two states were in alliance to regain Fort Detroit and surrounding areas from the hands of the British.

The battle lines were drawn on June 18 with the outbreak of the War of 1812, which pitted the newly established United States against Great Britain, Canada, and Indian tribes, all vying for territorial rights. One of the biggest proponents of growth was Kentucky, which was eager to acquire more land to expand its borders westward. Entirely committed, Kentucky sent 2,000 men, mostly untrained in combat, to the disputed area, to do whatever it took to keep their land away from the enemies.

It was a rough start for the Americans, who were forced to surrender Fort Detroit to British Major General Henry Proctor on August 16. That defeat angered President James Madison, who immediately regrouped the troops to win Detroit back. General William Henry

Harrison was the new leader in charge of the army of the Northwest Territory, while Brigadier General James Winchester was second in command. The selection of Winchester generated skepticism from the beginning. He had fought the British once before during the Revolutionary War, but his age now—sixty-one—was a factor. Many considered him inept and unpopular, unable to garner respect from his troops. Nevertheless, he accepted the position and vowed to forge ahead.

The two men divided their duties. Harrison led his troops to Upper Sandusky, Ohio, while Winchester defied his boss's orders and, instead of staying in Perrysburg, escorted the group of mostly Kentuckians toward Frenchtown, a small area about twenty-five miles outside of Detroit, whose residents had been begging to be freed from the control of the British and Indians. Winchester explained his decision to change course in a letter to Harrison, stating that "nothing but progressive actions" would keep his men from leaving when their six-month enlistment period expired.

The area was now in the grip of winter, causing added difficulty for Winchester's ill-equipped troops. Food was becoming scarce. Clothing was not heavy enough for the bitterly cold temperatures. Many were becoming weary after several months away from home.

Dragging their equipment across the frozen Maumee River, the troops arrived on January 18 in Frenchtown (present-day Monroe), where they experienced their first taste of battle. They pulled off an easy victory, and their confidence levels rose as they devoured their rivals' plentiful food supplies.

Rumors circulated of a sizable impending counterattack back over the River Raisin; however, Winchester ignored them, convinced that the British would take several days to assemble their forces before they would be ready for a counteroffensive. He then ventured off on his own to spend the night in the comfortable quarters of

Colonel Frances Navarre, about a mile from the settlement. He took with him the full supply of extra gunpowder, leaving his 934 soldiers without sufficient security. Guards at the encampment were posted everywhere except the road heading north.

Surreptitiously, Major General Henry Proctor pulled together a brigade of more than 1,300 men: more than 500 British troops and 800 Indians, led by the highly esteemed Chief Roundhead and Chief Walk in the Water. Ever so quietly, in the middle of the night, they took their positions just five miles outside of Frenchtown, armed with full artillery and half a dozen cannons. As day broke the morning of January 22, the British soldiers and Indian warriors attacked the Americans, who were caught totally off guard.

Sound asleep at his friend's home, Winchester was awakened by the sound of rapid gunfire. He made a mad dash for the nearest horse and galloped to his shattered army. The opposition saw this as a golden opportunity and promptly captured Winchester, who ordered his soldiers to put down their arms. But the Kentucky militiamen were bent on finishing the fight, swearing that they would rather die on the battlefield than surrender.

The Battle of the River Raisin was the bloodiest ever seen in Michigan. The Americans suffered the greatest number of fatalities, with more than 300 dead. Nearly 100 more were wounded, and more than 500 were taken prisoner. On the British side, 24 were killed, and some 160 were wounded. There were no reports on the number of Indian casualties.

General Proctor threatened to murder all the wounded and to set the whole town ablaze if a compromise surrender was not agreed upon. Grudgingly, the Americans gave in, and it appeared that the war was over.

Yet another surprise was waiting. As Proctor, fearful that American reinforcements would soon arrive, was marching his men and many of the able-bodied prisoners back to Detroit, the Indians had a plan of their own. At approximately ten o'clock the next morning, hundreds of Indians overran Frenchtown, violating the terms of surrender. They stormed into buildings housing the wounded, pillaged all their belongings, and then killed them. Severely wounded men clung to their beds as the Indians set the buildings on fire. The outside world listened as ear-piercing screams rang out. The brutality continued for hours. Those prisoners who survived were forced to walk to Fort Malden, where according to one survivor, Elias Darnell, "the road was, for miles, strewed with the mangled bodies."

More than sixty of the injured were killed in what one newspaper, the *Niles Weekly Register,* called "the most horrid assassination and cold-blooded butchery ever committed, or suffered to be done, by civilized man."

The unforgettable "River Raisin Massacre"—with its battle cry "Remember the Raisin"—had ended.

General James Winchester was eventually released and assigned to a new command; however, in regard to the lost battle, he asserted to the end that the loss wasn't his fault because he made no material mistakes that would be chargeable to him. Historical evidence may beg to differ.

STOMACHING A
MEDICAL DISCOVERY

1822

On the unseasonably cool day of June 2, 1822, business was bustling inside the American Fur Company on Market Street. Throngs of jovial voyageurs and clerks were trading fur pelts and repartee while the Indians quietly looked on. A single loud popping sound silenced the crowd as a young man fell to the ground. Blood gushed out of his stomach, and the local doctor was immediately summoned.

William Beaumont, a thirty-seven-year-old army surgeon stationed at Fort Mackinac, was on the scene with his medical kit, so sparsely equipped that it didn't even contain a thermometer. None was needed, though, as there was no question in his mind that the man's wound was life-threatening and that any attempt to save his life would have been useless. Beaumont was certain that the injured fellow would be dead within twenty minutes.

Two men had been comparing their duck-hunting equipment when one of their guns had gone off, accidentally hitting twenty-eight-year-old Alexis St. Martin from a distance of about three feet.

At such close range, the skin around the bullet's point of entry was badly burned, leaving an open hole the size of an adult hand. Protruding from the wound was a portion of his lungs, which Beaumont described in his journal "as large as a turkey's egg," caught on a sharp fragment of a rib. Whatever he had eaten for breakfast was now on its way out through the hole, too. In all, it was a gruesome sight.

Even though Beaumont wasn't officially a certified doctor, he had seen many things in his few years on the island, but this was undoubtedly the worst. Dr. Beaumont, as he could technically be called, received his training not through a fancy medical school, but by means of a one-year apprenticeship with a doctor in Vermont, a practice quite common in that era. Any additional education came mostly by administering on-the-job care to those in need.

Despite the severity of St. Martin's injuries, Beaumont dressed the wound with a carbonated poultice and clipped a bit of the rib with his pen knife to get the lung back inside. All this was done without the benefit of any painkillers. Surely this victim was from hearty stock. His survival was mind-boggling as the doctor witnessed him fight off both pneumonia and a worrisome cough within the first twenty-four hours.

Over the next few months, St. Martin's body began expelling whatever debris had entered it along with the gunshot, including pieces of the patient's own cartilage. Taking copious notes, Beaumont noted, "They continued to come away every five or six days until five were discharged from the same opening, the last three inches in length."

The body was healing beautifully, but the wound itself wasn't. No matter what was tried, the gaping hole in St Martin's stomach just wouldn't close. An operation appeared to be the only solution, to which St. Martin emphatically responded, "No, you will never operate on me." Reluctantly, Beaumont acquiesced and covered the cavity with linen compresses.

The county commissioners had been following the case keenly, and with the recuperation proceeding well, they decided it was time to take the patient off the "pauper" roles and return him to his native Montreal. The doctor was outraged that they would even think about sending St. Martin on a 2,000-mile journey in an open canoe. Surely, that would be the kiss of death, and Beaumont couldn't sit by and watch that happen. On a salary of $40 a month, the doctor could always use an extra hand with odd jobs around the house. And since the trapper could no longer work in that capacity, the situation appeared to be a perfect fit for both of them.

Thinking of this as a golden opportunity to conduct potentially history-making research, Beaumont began using his new houseguest as a guinea pig. By now, the tissue surrounding the opening had attached itself to the tissue on St. Martin's side, exposing his stomach permanently with the creation of a gastric fistula.

Recognizing the importance of this, Beaumont wrote, "I can look directly into the cavity of the stomach, observe its motion, and almost see the process of digestion. I can pour in water with a funnel and put in food with a spoon, and draw them out again with a siphon. . . . I might introduce various digestible substances into the stomach and easily examine them during the whole process of digestion."

One by one, the doctor placed various foods on a silk string and then lowered them into the hole in order to observe the stomach's reaction. St. Martin didn't seem to experience any pain as Beaumont inserted things like "highly seasoned a la mode beef, . . . raw salted lean beef, . . . boiled, salted beef, . . . stale bread, and a bunch of raw, sliced cabbage."

Beaumont's findings proved that other theories about digestion were incorrect. He discovered that the stomach, rather than grinding or fermenting food, digested it with the aid of gastric juices. A chemical reaction caused by acid in the juices actually was responsible for breaking down nourishment. Sometimes St. Martin would become irritated when the food was removed from his stomach; this reaction led Beaumont to deduce that anger can inhibit digestion. Among his other findings were that vegetables are more difficult to digest than meat or cereal and that milk coagulates before the digestive process begins.

The two men had a tumultuous relationship that went on for years. Several times St. Martin would get up and leave without telling anyone where he was going. Beaumont would frantically search for him and eventually bring him back.

St. Martin went on to father seventeen children, before passing away on June 24, 1880, at the age of eighty-six. He had miraculously survived fifty-eight years with a see-through stomach that brought advanced knowledge on digestion that remains unsurpassed today.

At the time of St. Martin's death in St. Thomas de Joliette, Canada, his children were concerned that his body might be perceived as a sideshow, so they allowed it to decompose for several days before burying their father's corpse eight feet below ground in an unmarked grave.

TOLEDO WAR

1835

No one in Michigan Territory believed that the struggle for state-hood would become so difficult that it would end up in a war. Yet under the leadership of the young, feisty, and politically savvy Stevens T. Mason, that's exactly what happened.

Appointed territorial secretary at age nineteen when he was too young to even vote, Mason, originally from Virginia, was passionate about getting Congress to approve statehood for Michigan. When the first petition for statehood failed in 1832 because the population was too small, he commissioned a census, discovering that there were 86,000 people living in the Lower Peninsula alone, far more than the required 60,000.

But when it came time to acknowledge the boundaries for the proposed new state, the real trouble began. On December 11, 1833, when Mason made the official application for statehood, his request riled congressmen from Ohio, who claimed that Michigan was taking some of the land that really belonged to them. When Ohio had been granted statehood in 1803, its northern boundary included

Toledo and all of the Maumee River, desirable for its waterway access, which would inevitably attract more settlers and more business. However, according to the Northwest Ordinance of 1787, the Toledo Strip rightfully belonged to Michigan.

So who really owned Toledo? Congressional tempers were flaring on both sides of the debate. Former President John Quincy Adams, now a Massachusetts congressman, was strongly in favor of Michigan's claims, stating during national legislative hearings in Washington, D.C., "Never in the course of my life have I known a controversy of which all the right [is] so clearly on one side and all the power so overwhelmingly on the other." But Ohio's voice was so loud in opposition that Michigan's admission to the Union was temporarily put on hold.

It began as a war of words. Ohio Governor Robert Lucas was adamant in his refusal to negotiate. Then he provoked even more anger by naming the county in which Toledo sat after himself. Mason fought back by making it a criminal offense for Ohioans to execute any official business in the Toledo Strip (now part of Lucas County), with a punishment of a $1,000 fine and/or a maximum of five years of hard labor.

Egos became uncontrollable, and a declaration for all-out war was issued. Ohio's legislature established a military budget of $300,000. Not to be outdone, Michigan countered with a war allocation of $315,000. On March 31, 1835, Governor Lucas led 600 armed troops to Perrysburg, just south of Toledo. Shortly afterward, Mason marched an army of 1,000 to the center of the city. The *Toledo Gazette* described the Michigan soldiers as "composed of the lowest and most miserable dregs of the community . . . low drunken frequenters of grog shops, who had been hired at a dollar a day." The nasty barbs continued while both groups were poised and ready for battle.

But there never was a real battle. The Michigan soldiers merely fired a few gunshots over the heads of the "enemy." Yet the power struggle continued well into the summer. A headcount in Ohio of 10,000 anxious volunteers was countered by Michigan's news outlets challenging the Ohio "million" to cross the boundary lines at their own risk as they would be "welcomed to hospitable graves."

The bitterness between the opposing sides grew as the threats continued to increase for several months. Lawsuits were filed constantly as spies infiltrated enemy territory, with much shoving and pushing and a number of arrests. Among all the squabbling and animosity, there was no major bloodshed.

In July 1835 Michigan's Deputy Sheriff Joseph Wood paid a visit to the Ohio partisan, Major Benjamin Stickney, with an arrest warrant in hand. Stickney, with his three sons by his side, became violent, and Wood demanded that they all be taken into custody. That didn't sit well with Two Stickney (yes, that's his real first name), who had warned Wood earlier, "The day you set foot in Toledo, your life will be in danger." As the actual arrest was being carried out, Two Stickney grabbed a knife and jabbed it into the ribs of the sheriff.

Even though the knife didn't puncture Wood's lungs, plenty of blood gushed out, the first and only bloodshed of the Toledo War. Two Stickney, with a price on his head of $500, fled the scene. Michigan's pleas for his extradition fell on deaf Ohioan ears.

President Andrew Jackson was growing impatient with reports of all the bickering and unrest and decided to put an end to it all. He signed legislation that would permit Michigan to become a state, but only after striking a deal giving Toledo to Ohio in exchange for 75 percent of the western Upper Peninsula, which was then part of Wisconsin. However, Michigan didn't find that arrangement equitable because, at the time, no one viewed the Upper Peninsula as anything more than a vast wasteland.

But the war had taken its toll on Michigan, which was now suffering financially. If it remained a territory, it wouldn't be able to receive any portion of the United States' current $400,000 budget surplus. So rather than continue with economic hardship, Michigan relented and decided to take the Upper Peninsula from Wisconsin in exchange for Toledo.

The angry, bitter, and very expensive Toledo War had ended, and on January 26, 1837, Michigan officially became the twenty-sixth state in the Union. While most people viewed the outcome as a major victory for Ohio, it was Michigan that had the last laugh. The expansive (9,000 square miles) and seemingly desolate Upper Peninsula turned out to be rich with timber and valuable copper and iron ore—resources that would all become profitable industries for many years.

In 1835 Stevens T. Mason, a member of the Democratic Party, was elected governor of Michigan at the age of twenty-four, becoming the youngest governor in the history of the United States. He served until 1840, and despite his young age, the "Boy Governor" made major long-standing contributions. A strong proponent of education, Mason in 1837 moved the University of Michigan from its original campus in Detroit to Ann Arbor, where it still stands today. Currently, there's a Mason Hall at both the University of Michigan and Michigan State University in East Lansing. The city of Mason, Michigan, is named after him, and yes, he finally received his own namesake county—Mason County, on the west side of the state. Quite a tribute to the strong-willed young man who led Michigan's only war.

DISCOVERING IRON ORE

1844

Shortly after Michigan gained statehood, Dr. Douglass Houghton, the state's first geologist, put a sign outside the government office that read something like this: HELP WANTED: AN INDIVIDUAL WITH EXCEPTIONAL SURVEYING SKILLS TO HANDLE THE DAUNTING TASK OF ACCURATELY PLOTTING OUT A NEWLY ACQUIRED MASSIVE WASTELAND. WORK WILL BE PERFORMED ENTIRELY IN THE UPPER PENINSULA, A SPARSELY POPULATED AREA WITH FOUR THOUSAND MILES IN NEED OF TOWNSHIP AND SECTIONAL LINES. ONLY THOSE WITH A KEEN MIND, ENDLESS DETERMINATION, AND A MINIMUM OF TWELVE YEARS OF EXPERIENCE NEED APPLY.

Just one man was perfectly suited for the position: William Austin Burt, who, along with his innovative solar compass, was about to make a dramatic discovery that would redefine the Upper Peninsula.

This position was viewed as an extremely difficult job, but Burt accepted the employment contract provided by Congress's $20,900 appropriation. He began assembling his team, which included his five sons, chainmen, axe men, and two Native Americans who would serve as packmen.

The team members journeyed north from Detroit on August 2, 1844, via the steamship *Illinois*. After two uneventful weeks on the Great Lakes, they arrived in their new "office," stocking a specially made flat-bottom boat with plentiful provisions. Their real task was only yet to begin.

The terrain they encountered was rugged, perhaps more than they had anticipated, and dotted with mosquito-infested swamps. The forests—dense with white pine, spruce, fir, and yellow birch—were hazardous to walk through.

As predicted, life in this environment was definitely not easy, and soon the stark reality of the wilderness set in. Even though it was only September, the weather—with chilly winds and the threat of snow—was becoming an issue. The men's food supply was rapidly diminishing, and they soon resorted to hunting. One night they killed three porcupines for dinner, cooking them over a burning tree stump. All the men were growing a bit weary, but Burt refused to let any of them turn around. He was a man with a tough work ethic, obsessed with accuracy, and intent on seeing this project to the finish. The surveying had to continue, no matter how hard life had become for all of them.

Burt routinely hiked through thorny brush, and even his clothing was feeling the effects. In a letter written to his wife, recovered years later by one of his descendants, he said that his "coat and pantaloons are most gone" and asked her to make him a new outfit out of the "strongest kind of bed ticking."

Hungry and bedraggled, the group managed to find a comfortable spot to camp for the night along the side of Teal Lake.

The next morning something different was in the air. On September 19, the men, awakening to beautiful clear skies, felt somewhat refreshed. It seemed like a promising day for everyone to fulfill the surveying schedule. The men gathered their equipment and were off to work. During their first mile of hilly landscape, compass man Harvey Millen noticed some bizarre behavior on his compass. The magnetic needle was spinning out of control. Baffled, he called for Burt, and together they observed that it was doing the exact opposite of what it should be doing. If they faced north, the needle shifted south. When they moved east, the needle pointed west. Something spectrally strange was upon them.

The team was hastily called together, and Burt commanded them to look around and see what they could find. Like scavengers, they combed the area, and each returned with a specimen of what had caused the violently whirling needle—iron ore. More specifically, it was an extremely high-quality iron ore made up of magnetite and hematite. The mystery was solved. They had discovered the expansive Marquette Range of iron ore.

Logically, a finding of this magnitude would have put a stop to the work at hand. But Burt didn't want to stop. For the next two days, he kept plugging along, until six inches of snow forced a major delay. At that point, it appeared that his surveying season was over, completing only 205 miles of the 4,000 miles that needed to be covered. Somehow that didn't really matter, since word of the amazing discovery was rapidly spreading across the country. To everyone's surprise, the Upper Peninsula, once thought of as barren, was fertile with rich natural resources.

Some were shocked when they learned that neither Burt nor any member of his team ever tried to make money from their breakthrough finding. The metal was deep inside heavy rock. Any process used to extract it would be extremely costly. It would be years before anyone actually turned a profit from the iron ore.

The next year, the hunt for additional iron ore was proceeding at a feverish pace. Ojibwa Indian Chief Marji-Gesick escorted a group from Jackson to the exact site of Burt's discovery. Eventually, that became the Jackson Mine, owned by the Jackson Mining Company, which was responsible for the growth of the city of Negaunee.

In 1845 Burt returned to the site with his supervisor, Douglass Houghton, who was so impressed that he forecast: "The bed of iron ore will compare favorably, both for extent and quality, with any known in our country." On a later trip with his sons, Burt stumbled upon another gem: fourteen beds of iron ore in the western section of what came to be known as the Menominee Range.

All told, one wacky little compass may have been the important ingredient to one of the country's largest mineral industries. The California gold rush that began in 1848 produced less than $1 billion worth of gold. Since William Austin Burt's discovery, the once-poor, lonely Upper Peninsula had an iron-ore industry worth an eye-popping $48 billion.

KENTUCKY RAIDS THE
UNDERGROUND RAILROAD

1847

The Underground Railroad was the ultimate metaphor in 1847: The conductors (men and women who provided the guidance and leadership for all operations) enabled the passengers, or cargo (slaves escaping from the South), to arrive in a timely fashion at their station (safe havens of temporary shelter) while on their way to the Promised Land (Canada). Southwest Michigan was a major player in what became a thriving philanthropic venture with the usual transportation components.

Behind the scenes, hundreds, possibly thousands, kept the Railroad running. All were firmly dedicated to delivering the fugitive slaves to freedom. Two main routes—one headed north from the Ohio River, the other from the Mississippi River—converged in Cass County, Michigan.

Vandalia, a residential community inhabited by a large number of Quakers, sits in the heart of the county. Religious social activists, the Quakers put their heart and soul into working to bring a new way of life to those who had been trapped in slavery.

Their efforts were highly secretive, and all transporting was done in covered wagons in the middle of the night. Conductors knew the name of the person at their next destination, but they never knew the identity of the person from the previous station. Conductors could identify each station by asking a code question, delivered precisely without even the slightest deviation: "Can you furnish entertainment for myself and another person?" If the person at the station answered "yes," then the conductors knew they had found a place of shelter, food, and safety for their passengers.

The Underground Railroad was highly dangerous for all involved. Every aspect of each trip was carefully measured to avoid the life-threatening consequences the fugitive slaves faced if they were caught. During their excursions, the fugitives would keep their eyes focused on the sky's northern lights so that they knew they were headed toward Canada, where slavery was illegal.

Between fifty and one hundred runaways felt so protected in southwest Michigan that they forfeited the rest of their "ticket" and decided to take up residence. They felt safe there, even with the possibility of their eventual discovery always lingering in the back of their minds.

Discussions among the townspeople were always guarded, and they were reluctant to openly acknowledge what they knew about the network. But a man named Carpenter was about to make a big dent in their confidentiality. Settling in nearby Kalamazoo, he walked into the office of Charles E. Stewart and announced that he wanted to study law. A professed abolitionist, he quickly made friends with the Quakers, who took him into their trust.

In reality, he was a spy from Bourbon County, Kentucky, which had seen more of its slaves run off than any other region in the South. Furious, the slaveholders were determined to stop at nothing to get their fugitive slaves back. With all of the hideaway homes clearly identified by Carpenter, a Kentucky brigade was ready to march into Michigan.

Thirteen headstrong Kentuckians, armed with weapons, rode in on a team of horses. Their targets were meticulously mapped out. In the darkest part of night, they swooped in on the property of Zachariah Shugart and captured one of their male slaves, who had been living in his own small cabin. But the man's wife managed to flee without being seen and immediately alerted neighbors of the impending danger.

The raiders proceeded next to the home of Stephen Bogue and ferociously pounded on the door, adamantly demanding to be admitted. Inside the house, the runaway slave recognized his former master's voice, inciting even more anger. Eventually the raiders broke down the door. After first resisting, the black man was beaten so badly that he surrendered.

Word of the seizures spread rapidly through the sleeping community. As the hot August day was breaking, one by one the abolitionists and their supporters managed to surround the Kentucky intruders, all of whom were armed with pistols, heavy clubs, and knives. A violent battle was brewing, quite a contradiction for the peace-loving Quakers.

By 9:00 a.m., the group had agreed to disagree with the help of the judicial system. It was quite a sight as the thirteen Kentuckians and their nine shackled slaves stormed up the courthouse steps, accompanied by at least three hundred abolitionists and sympathizers.

The judge listened to the arguments of both sides, even though it was unlawful for blacks to testify against any white person. It wasn't until the Fourteenth and Fifteenth Amendments to the Constitution were passed twenty years later that those rights would become legal. The Kentuckians were indicted on kidnapping, trespassing, and assault and battery charges. Their defense was that they were exercising their right to reclaim their property. They were able to produce a bill of sale for the slaves, but their downfall came when they couldn't provide a valid document showing that slavery was legal in the state of Kentucky.

The slave hunters were found guilty, and all the fugitive slaves who had been captured were immediately set free. News of the verdict spread like wildfire across the country, especially enraging citizens of Kentucky. Senator Henry Clay of Kentucky jumped to the Senate floor declaring Michigan "a hotbed of radical and renegades."

Six months later, the guilty southerners attempted to get their revenge. They filed suit in the U.S. District County Court in Detroit, hoping to reclaim the financial value of their former slaves. Legal proceedings went back and forth for several years, and finally in January 1851 the case was brought to trial, with nearly fifty witnesses called for each side. Despite all the time spent on all the legal wrangling, the trial ended in a hung jury.

Rather than face a retrial, a couple of the Quaker defendants gathered funds from the community and agreed to pay the plaintiffs $1,000, officially ending the case of the Kentucky slave owners versus the abolitionists. That amount of money took a hard toll. Some lost their farms, and others were in debt for years.

Reportedly, the $1,000 went to pay the plaintiffs' legal fees, so the slave owners never saw a penny of it.

ORPHAN TRAIN'S FIRST
HOPEFUL STOP

1854

On the banks of the Hudson River in New York City, the side-wheeler steamship *Isaac Newton* blew its "all aboard" whistle early on Thursday morning, September 28, 1854. Most of the passengers were smiling, but one group appeared noticeably subdued and expressionless. They were the thirty-seven boys and girls, ages six through fifteen, from the Children's Aid Society (CAS). All of them were orphans, chaperoned by Mr. E. P. Smith, headed to Michigan in hopes of finding a family that would adopt them. This was a historic journey: They were the very first riders on what came to be known for the next seventy-five years as the Orphan Train.

Life in the mid-1800s was difficult for many immigrant families in the East. There were too many mouths to feed with too little money. In some cases, hard labor took a deadly toll on the bread-winners, often leaving women as young widows with a number of children. Destitute and forsaken, youngsters were frequently abandoned by their parents and had to fight for their survival in the streets. Many of them turned to a life of petty crime, stealing food and other necessities.

The escalating problem came to the attention of Reverend Charles Loring Brace, a twenty-six-year-old Methodist minister who was determined to provide a better life for the thousands of homeless minors, whether they were officially declared orphans or had been deserted by their family. He founded the Children's Aid Society in New York City as a program to "help the children help themselves." But the numbers of children who needed help were overwhelming, and he soon realized there had to be alternative assistance. Like so many others of the time, he thought, "Go West," which is exactly where he took his experimental mission of "placing out" the children.

With the railroad in its infancy, transportation did not yet cross the continent to the Far West. Therefore, Brace set his sights on Michigan as the first placement center for orphans. Dowagiac, described by some as "a smart little town," was selected as the testing ground because of its rural setting and Christian values, and most likely because someone in town had a connection to Reverend Brace.

As the *Isaac Newton* docked in Albany at six o'clock the next morning, nine children who had arrived too late and missed the boat, literally, reunited with the CAS group. Interestingly, two boys who had sailed overnight were nonchalantly given to families on board, one to a merchant from Illinois and the other to a lady from Rochester who was "taking" him for her sister. Chaperone Smith knew the families for less than twenty-four hours, not enough time for any type of background check. Yet the two were now on their way with strangers to a virtually unknown new home.

During their time on the water, the children met a young stowaway named John, with scruffy clothes and hair so tangled that it appeared to have been matted for years. They begged and pleaded profusely with Smith, who again, without any knowledge of the boy's background, reluctantly added him to his roster of potential adoptees.

The train left at noon from Albany, and along their journey the children's eyes opened to a never-before-seen country, one filled with new discoveries like bright-yellow pumpkins. Wild with delight, they exclaimed, as one child later recorded in his diary, "Jist look at 'em! What a heap of mushmillons! . . . Do they make mushmillons in Michigan? . . . Won't we have nice things to eat? . . . Three cheers for Michigan!"

Overall, the trip in the freight cars had been strenuous for the little ones. After first heading to Detroit, followed by a transfer, they arrived at their destination at three o'clock Sunday morning. They were so weary and exhausted that they could barely stand, and many of them fell sound asleep on the platform. After breakfast, it was time to get ready for what had been called "the viewing." Those who made the trip had been thoughtfully selected for their appearance. Strong and muscular was a priority for the boys, sweet and dutiful for the girls. That way, it was believed, the young men could be of assistance on the farms, while the young women would be adept at household chores.

Inside the Presbyterian church in Dowagiac were the citizens who had gathered for their chance to take home one of the children. To advertise the children's arrival, posters had been strategically placed throughout town weeks in advance.

The posters read: "Homes for Children Wanted. A Company of Homeless Children from the East will arrive on Sunday, October 1. These children are of various ages and of both sexes, having been thrown friendless upon the world. They are well disciplined, having come from various orphanages. The citizens of this community are asked to assist the agent in finding good homes for them."

On the church's altar, seated in orderly fashion with the tallest in the back, were the forty-five spruced-up children now ready for adoption. None of them had any type of records, There were no birth certificates and no information on any medical history. Families came forward to check them over, touching their arms and legs to test for strength, and even putting their fingers inside their mouths to examine for teeth and jaw structure. One little boy later wrote in his journal, "I did everything I could to keep from biting that hand."

After several days, most of the children were "placed out" as Reverend Brace had hoped. But many brothers and sisters were not adopted by the same family and had to be forcibly taken to their new homes, screaming and crying as they were separated from their siblings.

The nine youngest orphans, who sat with tears silently rolling down their tiny cheeks, were never chosen. They had spent a week in Dowagiac without any family selecting them for adoption. It was time to again board a train with Mr. Smith, who escorted them to Iowa City in hopes of finding a new family there.

Records show that between 1854 and 1927 some 12,500 orphans rode the train to Michigan and were placed in cities all over the state, though most were never formally adopted. In total, during the CAS's existence, a quarter million children were put in new homes across the country as part of this "social experiment."

Of that precedent-setting Orphan Train, with its thirty-six placements in Dowagiac, whatever records may have existed are long gone, leaving no way to learn what became of any of that wide-eyed group once so excited to see their first Michigan "mushmillon."

ASSASSINATING A "KING"

1856

When James Jesse Strang first laid eyes on Big Beaver Island in the mid-1800s, he knew this was the next best place to heaven. Sitting proudly in Lake Michigan, some thirty-two miles off the shores of the northern Lower Peninsula, the secluded property had all the attributes he needed: plenty of land that could be planted, dense forests for building, and a host of fish that could be caught right from the shoreline. He finally found the perfect location "where I will come to build my kingdom."

As a young boy, Jesse James (his real name, which he later inverted) always dreamed of being a king someday. When he was eighteen, he set his sights on becoming betrothed to the future Queen Victoria, who at the time was only twelve. In his journal, as a teenager, he wrote, "I have spent the day trying to contrive some plan of obtaining in marriage the heir to the English crown." Just a year later, his haughty attitude persisted: "I ought to have been a member of the Assembly or a Brigadier General before this time if I am ever to rival Caesar or Napoleon which I have sworn to."

A window of opportunity opened when the head of the Mormon Church, Joseph Smith Jr., was killed in 1844. Strang, a convert to Mormonism from the Baptist faith, declared that he had been the chosen one, the person who would now lead the Mormon empire on its upward path.

Two years later, the charismatic, articulate, and good-looking new leader arrived on Beaver Island (it, too, had had a partial name change) with a couple of thousand of his followers. Their collective presence was intimidating enough to chase off the other residents, most of whom were Irish.

With the island pretty much to themselves now, the so-called Strangites found it easy to live according to their own rules. Strang was certainly good at that, instituting polygamy not only as an accepted practice but as a mandatory requirement for all church elders, who had to have at least two wives. He soon added five wives to his harem. One of them, who had been his former secretary, originally posed as a man to avoid scandalous gossip.

Realizing his power over his followers, Strang began to make plans for his lifelong desire to be crowned as a king. A stage, draped with elaborately hand-painted cloths, was built to complement the tabernacle. His good friend, an actor by the name of George J. Adams, was enlisted to officiate. On July 8, 1850, nearly three hundred devotees were gathered for the pageantry.

At 10:00 a.m. the flashy ceremony began. The embellished curtain slowly rose to reveal James Jesse Strang seated on a carved wooden throne, dressed in full regalia, which included a sweeping red flannel robe and a two-foot-long wooden scepter. At the conclusion of the ceremony, Adams placed a cardboard crown on his friend's head, solidifying Strang's self-proclamation as "King of the Kingdom of God on Earth."

Soon afterward, trouble began, not only within his newly created monarchy but also with neighboring Mackinac Island. The two islands competed for the upper hand in trade and legislative control. Beaver Island won out in all instances, replacing Mackinac as the refueling stop for steamers and exporting more food and timber, and Strang was elected to the state legislature as representative for both islands.

Uneasiness continued to mount, and Strang's life was definitely in danger. On one of Strang's trips to Mackinac, a deputy sheriff tried to arrest him, hoping to fire a fatal shot. But his gun misfired, and Strang escaped over the side of the boat, only to be back in his legislative seat a few weeks later.

Ever power-hungry, he next set forth special rules for women to live by. All his female subjects were required to wear loose-fitting clothing that came down to their knees. Underneath, pantaloons, or bloomers, would be worn. While most women conformed, a few did not. Thomas Bedford took umbrage, and his wife dissented, throwing Strang into a rage. Bedford was proclaimed guilty of "endeavoring to incite to mischief and crime" and whipped thirty-nine times as punishment.

Bedford grew tired of the mandatory rules, insisting they must stop. He paired up with fellow rebel Alexander Wentworth, and together they proceeded to plot their strategy. On June 16, 1856, as the USS *Michigan* docked on Beaver Island, the captain sent word requesting a meeting with "King" Strang. As the unarmed ruler approached, two men jumped him from behind, firing three bullets that lodged in his head, cheek, and spine and then pistol-whipping him brutally. Just as quickly as they appeared, they were gone, hopping back on board to sail safely away.

When the pair arrived at Mackinac Island, they were taken into custody and "supplied whatever they needed for their comfort." After a few days, Bedford and Wentworth were released to a hero's reception, during which they were treated to some of the finer things like cigars and brandy. In the name of justice, they were brought before a local judge, who fined them each $1.25 for court costs before releasing them.

As for Strang, he clung to life for more than two weeks before succumbing on July 8, exactly six years after he had been crowned "king." News of his assassination brought out his opponents, who stormed Beaver Island. They evicted all the Mormons, who ended up in either Chicago or Detroit completely destitute, and set fire to the tabernacle. The angry mob riddled Strang's house with bullets and took all of the books from his library and hurled them into the streets. The scene grew even more repugnant as they killed all his chickens.

In one final act of defiance to the supposed reign of terror, they took possession of the print shop, where they ran off hundreds of copies of a proclamation that read: "The dominion of King Strang is at an end." The only monarchy ever to have existed in the United States had been toppled—and with an extremely low probability of ever returning again.

BATTLE OF MANTON

1882

People go to battle over many things, some of them rather strange. The most common reason is to claim territory as well as the newly added power that comes with it. And if you stretch your imagination a bit, that was almost the case in 1882 when the small town of Manton, originally called Cedar Creek, engaged in a spirited confrontation with Cadillac, formerly known as Clam Lake, over the right to be the home of the county seat.

When it came time for each of Michigan's eighty-three counties to have their county seats designated, the decisions were amenable, at least for the most part. Usually, a city centrally located within the county or one of the largest cities was selected as the "capital" of the county. Most people don't visit the county seat on a regular basis—except to get a birth, marriage, divorce, or death certificate—and don't consider the county seat a particularly important place.

The people of Wexford County, however, viewed things a bit differently. They felt that being named the county seat was highly prestigious and would do almost anything to obtain the much-coveted honor. Late in 1872, it became a heated three-way competition among Sherman (previously called Manistee Bridge and the current holder of the county seat title), Cadillac, and Manton. A decade of contentiousness, pitting one town against the other, was officially under way.

Through backroom bargaining, wheeling and dealing, and some out-and-out lies, the trio kept clawing for position. A public vote was taken in April 1881, and Sherman lost what was now considered to be a very valuable county seat. Manton won the honor handily, 1,109 to 146, and rejoiced with wild antics and all-night partying. Clearly, it was one happy place, at least for the next year.

Exactly twelve months later, on April 4, 1882, another vote was taken, and the pendulum swung the other way. This time Cadillac, located in the extreme southeastern corner of Wexford County and more populated, held the upper hand, winning 1,363 to 309, but not without controversy and stubbornness on both sides. A couple of smaller towns were accused of destroying ballots, leaving open the possibility of a lawsuit. Manton officials threatened their own lawsuit aiming to ban Cadillac from removing government records.

But it was too late. The very next day, Wexford County Sheriff Charles Dunham, along with twenty of his finest deputies, boarded a train for the twelve-mile trip north to Manton. Bent on getting their hands on the county records, they made a mad dash into enemy territory, absconding not only with all the paperwork but most of the furniture as well. Instantly the entire area was abuzz with word of the infiltration. The townspeople flocked to the courthouse, and although they were not able to recover the paperwork, they forcefully rescued the money safes from capture. In thirty minutes the "robbery" was over, and the sheriff's team hopped back on the train. The Mantonites said the posse had "fled back to Cadillac in fear."

This was serious business now, with city pride at stake. So the sheriff surreptitiously devised a plan that would involve an "army" of reinforcements to accompany his "invasion." This attack would involve five hundred of Cadillac's finest, including lumberjacks, mill hands, and musicians. Their weapons: rifles, clubs, poles, crowbars, at least one broom, and, of course, the tubas from the brass band, playing the year's popular "Skater's Waltz." They were a motley crew, to say the least—wearing colorful plaid shirts, baggy overalls, loose-fitting suspenders, topped off with some cockeyed hats and a few shots of liquor—but they were ready for the Battle of Manton.

As with most stories, there are always two sides. Here is where the two versions diverge, depending on which city you believe. The Cadillac contingent, calling themselves the "First Volunteer Regiment, Cadillac Militia," swore that their intentions were honorable and that they meant no harm to anyone; only out of necessity were they defending themselves when met head-on by "every able-bodied citizen of Manton." They claimed that Manton brought out every man, woman, and child on the offense, doing their part to try to harass the "Cadillackers." Women were said to have gone to their kitchens, gathered all the chicken fat, lard, and butter they could find, and then greased the railroad tracks so that the train was unable to move.

Contrary to that, the townspeople in Manton said that their town was approached by a drunken sheriff and a drunken clerk leading a crowd of five hundred to six hundred men, all of them inebriated, returning to seize their county records. To shield their property, they barricaded the courthouse, since they claimed that their enemies had ordered it to be demolished. At that point, the sheriff sicced his "troops" on the people of Manton "like a pack of crazed hounds," and they shattered the windows, ripped out the documents, and bolted back to Cadillac.

Whichever side you choose to believe, the story has the same ending: Cadillac won the war and became (and still remains) the seat of Wexford County. The victors' excitement must have worn off quickly, since they didn't start building their courthouse until 1911.

With the passing years, no one is quite sure if any injuries befell either city. Some say that a Manton man was murdered and buried with the hatchet still solidly set in his chest. Others say that a pack of drunken twelve-year-olds ran rampant through the streets, battering innocent people. Whatever the case, both Cadillac and Manton saw a black eye or two, with a hint of the bruised feelings and animosity lingering to this very day.

LOGGING OUT OF A JAM

1883

Michigan's overabundance of lush forests was perceived as both a blessing and a curse. The imposing white pines provided solid shelter, yet clearing them to build a home was a rugged task. Often standing as much as two hundred feet in height and five feet in diameter, the trees could be overpowering. Folklore has it that Michigan forests were so thick a squirrel could travel five hundred miles without touching ground.

Until the 1840s the trees were viewed almost as a nuisance. But then some forward-thinking entrepreneurs thought, "Why not cut down the trees and create a new industry?" Soon, potential land barons, many of them from the East, raced to seize as many forest-rich acres as they could afford. The lumbering industry in Michigan began as a small seed and blossomed into a full-fledged lucrative enterprise.

During the fall and winter, lumberjacks and loggers were busy chopping down as many of the state's hearty trees as their axes and saws could handle. The onset of winter provided the optimal time for all the trees to be placed along the riverbanks, almost in a state of hibernation, waiting for the arrival of spring, when they would be placed in the river to float to sawmills. The placement of the logs was an intense and often dangerous job, requiring workers to put in eighteen-hour days standing in ice-cold water.

Despite the hazards, lumbering during the summer of 1883 seemed to go pretty much on schedule, even though the previous year's dry spell had produced an unusually high number of logs that had been harvested. But then the torrential rains and violent storms came. So much rain had fallen that the water levels had risen to record highs of twenty inches over flood stage. The enclosures that grouped the logs together, called booms, became stressed to the breaking point. It was now evident that a looming threat was about to become real.

On June 26, a trio of piledrivers, hired to steer the logs in the water, asked for two vacation days so that they could enjoy the Barnum circus in Muskegon. Their boss quickly responded negatively, saying he needed every one of them to be in town since it appeared that the Grand River was going to overflow at any minute. His predictions were accurate. As rain continued to fall, the river climbed another eight inches by July 24. Two days later, a major boom holding 50 million board feet of logs broke, causing the Grand River to jam like never before, with logs piled some thirty feet deep, extending for more than seven miles. The weight of the wet wood caused so much pressure that the Detroit, Grand Haven and Milwaukee Railroad Bridge caved in, toppling over from a height of more than a hundred feet before sinking. It wasn't long before three more bridges collapsed.

Reports in the Grand Rapids *Daily Democrat* provided a vivid description: "Following the broken spans of the bridge came the great mass of logs like a monster demon mad and bent on destruction. The logs groaned and pitched in every conceivable shape in a mad chase through the breath. Wherever the water was visible at point[s] here and there, it seethed and boiled and foamed like the whirlpool at Niagara."

This nightmarish scene needed to be fixed immediately. Otherwise, 150 million board feet of lumber, weighing approximately 37 million tons, could break loose from the massive boom near Stearns Bayou and end up in a wild frenzy in Lake Michigan, never to be recovered.

This was the biggest logjam in the country's history, and if it entered the Great Lakes, it could permanently cripple the area's economy. Millions of dollars' worth of lumber would be lost, likely bankrupting many sawmills. The banks that had loaned money to the sawmills would lose everything. Countless numbers of people would be out of work. And with the bridges gone, the railroad might never be able to recover, cutting off transportation between the two sides of the state.

With so much at stake, there was no time to waste. First, an on-the-spot decision needed to be made as to how to relieve the pressure of the logs now inextricably tangled together. Would an axe, a peavey, dynamite, or the labor-intensive placement of pilings work best?

Seventy-five courageous men were called in to work around the clock to drive pilings into the river's floor. Every so often a log would succumb to the pressure of those behind it and would fly into the air as if propelled by a slingshot, putting many of the men's lives in danger.

Canadian-born John Walsh, who had lost one of his arms years ago, was selected to lead the crews. Operating a steam-powered pile driver, he masterminded a plan that would selectively, and hopefully correctly, place clumps of sixteen piles, each aimed at redirecting pressure toward the riverbank. An unflappable leader not to be deterred, Walsh responded to an intruder who refused to leave the scene by knocking him overboard into shallow water. When the man didn't surface, Walsh used his iron hook arm to fish him out, throwing him on the bank unconscious, and then went back to work.

The crew continued working for four days nonstop. The most treacherous time was at night, when it was virtually impossible to identify where a spot might break loose, causing massive destruction.

Soon the extent of the problem became clear. The biggest challenge now was the flood itself, which didn't have an outlet because of the enormous weight of the logs tightly stacked down to the river's bottom. It appeared that the only way to alleviate this problem was to quickly dig another channel, in hopes that the onslaught of logs would be diverted to the new opening.

With this new auxiliary channel in place, the logjam was broken, and the timber began to flow again in a controlled fashion through the Grand River, avoiding a near crisis in Lake Michigan. The community was able to breathe a bit easier.

John Walsh, a marine engineer with the foresight and determination to create the barriers and auxiliary channel, was recognized as the hero who saved both the timber industry and Michigan's economy. For his heroism, he was awarded a gold watch etched with a pile driver, which today is a property of Grand Haven's Tri-Cities Historical Museum.

THOUSANDS VOWING "I DO"

1907

Early on Thursday, July 18, 1907, John R. Schays, age nineteen, and Ethelyn M. Yeargen, age eighteen, both from Chicago, stepped up to the counter and bought two tickets to travel to Michigan on the popular *Roosevelt Steamboat.* That single action was the start of an event that would change their lives forever.

In the early 1900s strains of live music greeted the crowds of young couples disembarking at the bustling boat dock in St. Joseph. The song most commonly played was Richard Wagner's bridal chorus from the opera *Lohengrin,* today known as "Here Comes the Bride." Couples like John and Ethelyn flocked to tie the knot in this western Michigan town, which for a quarter century deservedly held the title of "Wedding Capital of the Midwest."

Because of its alluring charm and Michigan's relatively lax marriage requirements, St. Joseph became the wedding site of choice for those coming from out of state, mainly from Chicago. In 1897 the state adopted a policy of secret marriage, allowing people to be legally married without anyone else knowing about it. Rather than being recorded in some government office, the official marriage certificate instead was presented directly to the couple. The only other legal proof was hidden in a file with the judge and then permanently sealed for all eternity.

Besides secret marriage, Michigan had all the trappings to become the perfect express wedding destination: the absence of any residency restrictions; no public posting of any announcement; no family witnesses required (the local clerk and his wife would suffice, or anyone else plucked off the street); and the added bonus that the permissible age for getting married—just eighteen—was the lowest of any nearby state.

Starry-eyed and in love, young couples would hop on the original love boat, a St. Joseph–bound steamer, where they could hold hands and dreamily gaze into each other's eyes throughout the duration of the four-hour trip. For some inexplicable reason, Sunday was the favorite day, enabling them to leave Chicago in the morning, quickly get married, and then return home that evening as husband and wife. It was a *fait accompli* before their parents had any idea of what was going on.

Demand for the weekend weddings grew to overload capacity. More steamboats were added to the route, and police security was brought in "to restrain the bridal couples from pushing each other into the Chicago River in a frenzied effort to get into the boat," as the *Chicago Tribune* wrote. As the future husbands and wives scurried off the boat, hordes of onlookers were there to greet them, most of them simply nosey, treating the occasion as one would a spectator sport. Perhaps that's why John Schays chose midweek for his wedding: to avoid all the crowds and to allow him a couple of extra days for his honeymoon.

Once on land, the young couple made the familiar mad dash to the Berrien County Courthouse to fill out the mandatory paperwork. Next, they had to apply for their marriage license. For a fee of $2, they would be issued a standard, unadorned license. But for an extra 50 cents, they could choose a much more ornate folder adorned with a picture of Cupid shooting his bow and arrow or some sweet romantic verses.

Officiating at weddings was big business for both the justices of the peace and the clergy. Some even went so far as to advertise with handbills that were passed out on the steamers, stating "Matrimonial Headquarters at St. Joseph. . . . Will Attend to all the Details if You Furnish the Bride, Licenses Issued and Ceremony Performed any Day of Week—Day or Night." It was a round-the-clock operation, with the clerk on occasion being awakened at two in the morning to perform his duties.

John had decided that a justice would be fine. After he submitted all the required information, his "case" was assigned to Judge Freeman Evans. Both he and his bride were dressed in their finest clothes and clinging to each other as they stepped forth for the short ceremony.

By their sides stood their witnesses, James B. Nisbot and Mabelle Walker, both from Chicago. It's not certain whether either of them knew the engaged couple or whether they were just two people John and Ethelyn met on the boat. As a matter of convenience, James and Mabelle might have even been the next two in line to get married, as it was fairly common for the courts to arrange for the best man and maid of honor. On the occasion of the midnight marriage, the clerk's wife and whoever else was in the household at the time would serve as the official observers.

Standing somewhat awkwardly in the judge's chamber, without any music, flowers, or other customary pomp and circumstance, the judge asked John the all-important question: "Do you take this woman to be your lawfully wedded wife?" Similarly, Ethelyn was questioned for her response. After each replied with the appropriate "I do," the judge pronounced them husband and wife. The groom kissed the bride, the two-minute ceremony was over, and the new Mr. and Mrs. John Schays exited in wedded bliss. It was customary for these long-distance marriages to be short and to the point. The faster the turnover, the more money for the presiding official. Reportedly, the record for the speediest merger was an eye-blinking thirty seconds.

Afterward, the newlyweds likely spent some time in St. Joseph, helping to boost the local economy by spending money on food and lodging. The lightning-speed weddings appeared to be a win-win situation for all concerned, except the secretary of state, who took issue with "the development of the famous St. Joseph marriage industry."

Signaling his displeasure to the state government, Governor Alexander Groesbeck took a major step toward permanently silencing the wedding bells for out-of-towners. On April 30, 1925, he signed a new statute that would require a five-day waiting period after the license application. His romantic side came out, though, when he said it wouldn't go into effect until August 27, giving all the summer brides plenty of time for their last-minute nuptials. By that time, hopefully, Mr. and Mrs. Schays would have been preparing to celebrate their eighteenth wedding anniversary.

FURNITURE STRIKE OF 1911

1911

In the late 1800s Grand Rapids had the perfect environment for the burgeoning furniture industry: immense forests with endless quantities of lumber, a railroad system for quick transportation of goods, and an influx of immigrants from across the ocean. As one of the first furniture companies stated, "You put a log in one end and it comes out the other as a chair."

Furniture makers began popping up all over the area. By 1881 explosive growth in the industry led to the formation of the Grand Rapids Furniture Association (GRFA), uniting shop owners in what became the first furniture advocacy group in the United States. The railroads knew a good thing when they saw it and began raising rates on the popular but uncompetitive route between Chicago and Grand Rapids. So the GRFA stepped in, negotiating fair transportation costs for everyone.

Business was booming. There wasn't a stadium seat or a school desk in the country that didn't feature the handiwork of a Grand Rapids worker. By the turn of the twentieth century, Grand Rapids had clearly earned its title as "Furniture Capital of the World."

With an upsurge in production came growing employee discontent. Various ethnic groups—Dutch, Swedish, German, and Norwegian—were among those filling the ranks of skilled labor. It wasn't long before they realized they needed some negotiating power of their own. In 1886 the furniture workers went on strike for the first time. Surprisingly, they weren't asking for more money but rather wanted to work fewer hours for the same pay. The workers' demands didn't go over well with the owners, leading to a work stoppage from March until June. Families quickly became hungry, and the workers soon returned to their crafts without any change in their work status.

In the spring of 1900, the Amalgamated Wood Workers International Union (AWWIU) came to Grand Rapids for its national convention, hoping to attract new members. Sixty-eight Germans spent a week listening to the rallying cries during organizational sessions, compared with the four hundred who sampled beer during the social session. The AWWIU didn't succeed in unionizing locally, although its presence was clearly felt.

In the following decade, furniture manufacturers demanded more and more labor at cheaper and cheaper costs. The next wave of immigrants, from Poland and Lithuania, was happy to oblige. By 1910 there were more than 7,200 furniture workers, and it was not uncommon to find twenty different languages spoken in a single factory. Owners responded by dividing work areas according to nationality, also easing animosities among the groups.

No matter what ethnicity, the workers all shared the same goal of owning their own home and establishing a better life for their families. They soon learned, however, that other industries across the country were giving their employees slight annual pay raises, but the furniture business in Grand Rapids hadn't increased wages at all in five years. Unrest began to set in.

Workers at the time averaged $1.91 for an eleven-hour day. In an early example of gender discrimination, boys between fourteen and sixteen earned 89 cents a day, while girls of the same age made only 75 cents a day. By December an increasingly volatile work environment led cabinetmakers to come forward and demand a nine-hour workday, more money, and an end to the practice of pay per piecework. After they staged a brief walkout, their manager told them to return to their jobs, assuring them that at the beginning of January their demands would be met.

It didn't happen. In fact, none of their requests were granted, making matters even worse, and workers began to grumble. Tempers were simmering amid numerous accusations that rebellious and uncooperative employees were being blacklisted. Arbitration was posed as a possible means of settlement, but the manufacturers rebutted that "questions that struck at the very vitals of the industry could not be submitted to arbitration."

For months, barbs were exchanged between the Carpenter's District Council and the Furniture Manufacturer's Association, with nothing accomplished. Neither side was willing to budge. It became clear that a strike was inevitable.

At 9:00 a.m. on April 19, 1911, Grand Rapids was brought to a standstill when thousands of employees walked off their jobs in fifty-nine factories. Everyone weighed in with an opinion, especially the clergy, who were quick to take a position. Most of the companies' owners were Protestant, and their churches, under the leadership of Fountain Street Church's pastor, Alfred Wisley Wishart, favored management. The workers, many of whom were eastern European and Catholic, were supported by Auxiliary Bishop Joseph Schrembs.

The demands remained the same: shorter hours, better working conditions, and a 10 percent pay increase. Workers also wanted the right to collective bargaining and the right to establish unions, further fraying nerves. During the strike, workers endured numerous hardships. Money was tight, and workers found it difficult to feed their families. Many workers, unable to make their mortgage payments, lost their homes to foreclosure. As the strike dragged on into the steamy summer, the workers' situation was getting grimmer and grimmer.

Still, neither side would budge.

For the most part, the strike was considered peaceful, until the manufacturers brought in strikebreakers. Some of the women scabs hid stones under their skirts, which they would throw at the picketers. The striking workers had the support of national unions, the Catholic Church, and the mayor. But by early August, the strike fund, which entitled workers to $5 each week, was almost depleted. Then the leaders of the popular Christian Reformed Church came out with an official decree that no worker who belonged to the church would be allowed to join a union.

That was the last straw. On August 19, the seventeen-week strike was over, and the workers, fatigued and beaten down, went back to work. They hadn't won any of their requests—there was no union, no right to collective bargaining. The owners appeared to have won.

But there was a newfound, respectful relationship. Owners knew that workers were capable of walking out and staying out. Over time, owners granted pay hikes and gave workers a fifty-five-hour workweek for sixty hours' worth of wages.

Afterward, the furniture industry enjoyed a period of prosperity, yet things never quite returned to the way they were before the strike. As it turned out, the work stoppage proved to be one of the most significant events in Grand Rapids' history: The strict demarcation line between the city's white-collar Southeast and the blue-collar West Side endured for years to come.

SUMMER SPARK SETS TOWNS ABLAZE

1911

The summer of 1911 was hot, spelled with a capital *H*. The heat was so oppressive that a person would work up a sweat just opening the window to try to cool off. During the daylight hours of early July, the thermometer registered anywhere between 94 and 100 degrees, and that was in the shade.

People in the northeastern section of Michigan had long forgotten what a frigid winter felt like. The heat was so unbearable that a local newspaper put a cartoon on its front page depicting someone pounding on the gates of Hell and begging for admittance, saying, "I'm looking for a cool spot." The devil, flashing a fiendish grin, responds, "Come in quickly and close the door."

The twin cities of AuSable and Oscoda sat pleasantly surrounded by thick forests filled with the highly desirable white pine. Once, not long ago, their lumbering industries were so prosperous and their population was growing so quickly that they had been dubbed "Little Chicago" and "Young New York."

Because of the rich timber resources, it only made sense that everything in town was made of wood, right down to the sawdust and wood-chip streets and sidewalks. Residents never questioned the lack of cement thoroughfares, nor did they ever see how it could eventually become a major detriment.

Tuesday, July 11, was another day of unbearably scorching temperatures. For several days, a single forest fire had been lurking on the outskirts of town, but no one perceived it as a serious threat—that is, until winds started kicking up about two o'clock that afternoon. The 50-mile-per-hour wind swept the blaze into AuSable with lightning speed. Complicating matters was a train called the Lincoln Stub, which was passing through Oscoda: It accidentally threw off sparks from its engine, igniting a nearby lumber yard. In the torrid weather, all the wood acted as kindling, converting everything into an inferno. The fire jumped over the AuSable River. Intense flames took aim at all sides of the two towns, setting off a chain reaction of searing devastation.

In the first five minutes of the fire, twenty houses on Main Street went up in smoke. Within two hours, both towns had burned to the ground. The fire had ravaged everything in its wake, except four buildings in AuSable and twenty homes in Oscoda. People were frantically scrambling for shelter. Logically, the first route of escape was to the edge of Lake Huron, where men, women, children, and animals sought relief from the encroaching wildfires. A few people buried their precious silver pieces in the sand in hopes of retrieving them later. Most people, though, had left everything they owned behind.

The flames kept coming closer and closer to the shoreline, testing even the best swimmers' abilities. As children without any life preservers struggled in the water, a steamer appeared almost miraculously out of nowhere in the nick of time. The *Niko,* of the Edward

Hines fleet under the command of Captain Meyer, pulled up to the dock and began rapidly loading 208 people on board. Two small fires broke out on the fore and aft as it drifted out to sea, but they were quickly extinguished. After a harrowing experience, all passengers arrived at the nearest safe harbor of Bay City.

One of the first escapees was sixty-five-year-old Jennie Mead, who told a reporter from the *New York Times,* "I was home alone when the fire reached our town. It kept getting nearer and nearer home, and finally when I had just about given up hope of being taken care of, the neighbors were so excited, my son rushed in and carried me out to a safe place on the sand."

Some of those remaining in town were not as fortunate. Five people perished, all from excruciating burns. Considering the intensity of the flames, many were surprised that the loss of life was so small. About a thousand people were left homeless, with nothing except the clothes on their back. Michigan Governor Chase Osborn sent out a plea for all citizens to contribute whatever they could—clothing, food, shelter, or money—to the survivors. The episode brought out the best in people, bonding them together in the worst of times.

The destruction of physical property was more widespread than anyone could have ever imagined. In the small town of Tower (population eight hundred), 113 miles to the north, nearly all of the businesses were destroyed. The Bay City Fire Department was called in to help save the tiny town of Waters, but the firefighters arrived too late to save the Stephenson Lumber Company, valued at $400,000. Alpena asked for their aid, too, but the firefighters were delayed on the train, resulting in another half-million-dollar loss. Also affected were Onaway and Millersburg. Hit the hardest was H. M. Loud Sons Company in Oscoda, which owned a variety of mills and lumber yards worth an estimated $1.5 million.

Railroads came to a screeching halt, as the heat of the fires had warped their tracks. One passenger train on the Detroit to Mackinac line was able to maneuver its way through the towns by running on an old section of track used by the lumber industry. Passengers reported flames shooting a hundred feet into the air, scorching the sides of the cars and cracking the windows.

The fires' aftermath was devastating. The financial toll was in excess of $3 million. Most cities would never fully recover, and charred buildings sat as eyesores. It was too painful to think of rebuilding immediately.

By the time the last burning ember had been extinguished, it didn't matter where people had ended up or whether they ever recovered their buried treasures. They were happy simply to be alive and grateful to be able to take a deep breath of smoke-free fresh air.

ITALIAN HALL CATASTROPHE

1913

It was Christmas Eve 1913 in Calumet, the heart of copper country.
At homes across the area, young boys were spit-polishing their shoes
while little girls were putting on their prettiest dresses and adorning
their hair with curly ribbons. There was an air of excitement that
hadn't been felt here for quite some time.

Tensions had been mounting long before 15,000 miners went
on strike on July 23, 1913. Copper had been the area's main source
of prosperity for almost forty years. The work wasn't easy. Long,
twelve-hour days spent in darkness more than 1,000 feet into the
mine were beginning to take their toll. On the other hand, increasing competition from copper mines in the western United States
prompted companies to make major changes.

Workers wanted shorter hours, more pay, and safer conditions,
starting with the two-man drill, rather than the more dangerous one-
man drill the companies were now forcing them to use. Neither side
was willing to compromise, despite conflicts so violent that the governor called in all 2,000 members of the Michigan National Guard.

It had been five months since any of the miners had worked, leaving families despondent and financially strapped. But on this day, all that was forgotten as people readied themselves for the big Christmas party about to take place at the Italian Hall.

The celebration was the brainchild of Annie Clemenc, whose father and husband both worked in the mines. One of the most active protesters against the Calumet & Hecla Mining Company, "Big Annie" led daily marches through the streets, rallying thousands of followers. Standing six feet two inches tall and waving a ten-foot-high American flag, she was a woman to be reckoned with.

As president of the Western Miners Auxiliary No. 15, Annie was determined to make this Christmas the best she could for all of those who had already forsaken so much. She arrived early, with bags full of candy, and dressed the tiny five-foot stage with sparse decorations. At two o'clock, more than 175 men and women and 500 joyfully boisterous children scampered up the narrow flight of stairs to the Italian Hall's second floor and crowded into the large meeting room. There, the collection of Croatian, Finnish, and Italian immigrants sang Christmas carols, while forgetting about their pain and suffering. The children lined up in front of the stage with their hands eagerly stretched out as Annie gave each child as much candy as she could. When Santa Claus entered the room, the noise level had reached a feverish pitch. Santa took the stage to wild screams. The packed room was aglow with activity.

Then, almost on cue, the double doors at the top of the stairs burst open, and a man in a dark coat with a hat pulled down over his eyes leapt into the room and, in a loud booming voice, yelled "Fire." He stayed a few seconds, as if to be certain people heard him. Then, just as quickly as he appeared, he was gone. Instantly, the merriment turned to sheer pandemonium—chilling screams, frantic searches for an escape, parents trying to find their children, shouts of "Get to the doors."

The first few people through the doors made it safely down to the street. But in the height of the chaos, as more and more people filled the stairwell, someone fell, creating an instant domino effect. Bodies fell on top of bodies. Sisters fell on top of their brothers. Small children were crushed as fellow partiers stampeded over them. Others could not breathe as people toppled over them.

The stairwell was now a tightly packed pile of people six feet high, a horrific assemblage extending from the bottom of the stairs to the top, a total of some thirty feet. It took rescue teams hours to untangle the remains, and eventually they placed the corpses on tabletops where families could search for their loved ones. Frantic efforts to administer CPR were futile.

Within hours, emotions ranged from outrage to grief to incomprehension when it was learned that there had been no fire at all. A tragic melee had been caused by one false word uttered by a stranger. Who could have possibly played such a horrible trick?

An outpouring of sympathy, from both the strikers and those opposed to the strike, brought in donations of $25,000 to the heartbroken families. Every segment of the community felt the immeasurable pain of this malicious act. The local fire hall was transformed into a temporary morgue, accommodating all seventy-three of the deceased: eleven adults and sixty-two children, ages two to sixteen, many of them without any visible signs of trauma. Scores of others were injured.

When the coroner finished his three-day-long investigation, the findings were inconclusive, with no cause of death listed. Without a definitive conclusion, the culprit basically went free since none of the deaths were declared a homicide. Adding to the mystery was the questionable "loss" of the official coroner's report, which was missing for years.

The identity of the man who yelled "Fire" has never been discovered. Witnesses at the time claimed he was wearing a white pin with the words "Citizens Alliance," the group working to obstruct the strike. Was it someone who had had too much to drink? Extensive investigations that went on for years never yielded an answer.

And then there's the question of the doors. The doors at the bottom of the Italian Hall's stairs opened inward, causing the escapees to be trapped. Inward-opening doors were clearly in violation of the fire code, which said that doors must open outward. Observers say there was more to the story and swear that a poison gas permeated the air in the hall. Others say that some type of slippery material was placed on the stairs, forcing people to stumble and fall.

One thing is certain. Although a century has passed, the fascination with what's been called "the 1913 Massacre" still continues. The Italian Hall was purchased in 1945 by the Fraternal Order of Eagles for $3,200. It changed hands again in 1972 when it was sold to a local businessman for $2,000. Beyond repair, the hall was finally torn down in 1984. All that remains is a brick arch, under which a memorial plaque stands. It was dedicated on November 13, 1989, as a crowd gathered to sing a comforting chorus of "Silent Night," commemorating the peace that eluded Calumet on that Christmas years ago.

STORM OF 1913

1913

There's an old saying in Michigan: "If you don't like the weather, stick around for ten more minutes and it's sure to change." Weather in Michigan is highly unpredictable, especially in the volatile month of November, when almost anything can happen.

November is particularly unsettling for the Great Lakes and its shipping trade, which has become notorious for major tragedies. What's come to be known as the Armistice Day storm of November 11, 1940, is the worst on record for Lake Michigan, the only one of the Great Lakes not to have an international border. That day produced 75-mile-per-hour winds and waves up to twenty feet. The storm took down two large freighters, the *William B. Davock* and the *Anna C. Minch,* while another one, the *Novadoc,* ran aground. In total, fifty-nine lives were lost.

On November 18, 1958, gale winds brought down the *Carl D. Bradley,* a 639-foot limestone carrier, literally breaking it in half before it sank just off Gull Island in Lake Michigan. Thirty-three people, most of them northern Michigan residents, were killed.

The worst shipwreck of modern times inspired Gordon Light-foot's song "The Wreck of the *Edmund Fitzgerald*." High winds, blowing snow, and poor visibility off Whitefish Point in Lake Superior took down the 730-foot freighter and her entire twenty-nine-member crew on the night of November 10, 1975.

Since the mid-1800s at least twenty-five disastrous November storms have hit Michigan. Yet most historians would agree that the very worst of them was the Great Lakes Storm of 1913, so powerful that it has its own collection of memorable nicknames: "White Hurricane," "Freshwater Fury," "Big Blow." But if you mention just "The Storm" to mariners, they'll know what you're talking about.

One of the most unusual characteristics of this storm was its duration. The typical lifespan of a weather episode is somewhere between twenty-four and thirty-six hours. Not so the Great Lakes Storm of 1913. It began on November 7 and didn't wind down until November 12.

The morning of Thursday, November 6, 1913, began fairly routinely. Temperatures were unseasonably warm for that time of year, and Great Lakes shipping was hustling to get in one last trip before the onset of the winter season. Freighters were loaded down with materials such as coal, iron ore, or recently harvested grain.

But weather forecasting in that era was far from sophisticated. There were no Doppler radar systems to provide hourly predictions. Radio was still new, and few ship owners had it installed on their vessels. Not many people recognized the low-pressure system skirting the southern states while another low-pressure area and Arctic front were heading down from Canada. The two systems were heading to a major meteorological calamity, the likes of which these waters had never seen.

By Friday morning the temperatures had dropped drastically, by more than 30 degrees in some spots, and the air was now bitterly cold. The winds were picking up in intensity, and at 10:00 a.m. a storm warning was issued for the Great Lakes. The Coast Guard and weather stations hung out white pennants over square red flags with black centers to signal the severity of the upcoming storm. Not long after, the flags were all replaced with lanterns letting sailors know a hurricane was on its way.

Over the next twenty-four hours, the velocity of the winds began to skyrocket, with gusts more than 50 miles per hour on Lake Superior. That Saturday, Milton Smith, a seaman on the *Charles S. Price,* got the chills, literally, and decided to check himself off the 524-foot carrier. Reportedly, he had premonitions about something terrible happening to the ship and decided he didn't want to take any unnecessary risks. He attempted to convince his good friend and fellow seaman, Arz McIntosh, to walk off the job, too. Arz, however, desperately needed the job so that he could pay for an operation to repair his deteriorating eyesight. He told his buddy Milt that he wished he had more time so that he could leave with him. Instead, he decided to stick it out for one more trip. Bidding his fellow sailor farewell, he said that he'd see him again soon in Port Huron.

The storm reached maximum strength on Sunday, November 9. Although all the Great Lakes were affected, Lake Huron undoubtedly was hit the hardest. Sitting at the base of the lake is Port Huron, where winds were recorded gusting more than 70 miles per hour on land and more than 90 miles per hour on sea. In the midst of the wind, the rain started, followed by sleet, ice, and eventually snow. The blinding snow squalls also made it impossible for crews to walk on the decks, where the sailors would be painfully pelted with frigid ice. The storm had taken a violent turn, and it appeared that for the ships there was no turning back.

One after another, waves more than thirty-five feet high, taller than the ships, began thrashing the vessels. And the trouncing didn't let up. The raging gales went on, not for the usual four or five hours, but continuously for a full sixteen hours. This storm's fury was unrelenting.

Onshore, Port Huron was immobilized, with snow drifts four to five feet high. On the seas, the situation was far graver. News traveled much more slowly then, and the newspapers lagged in their reporting. At first, it was thought that all the ships may have been miraculously saved. But slowly, the sad truth was discovered.

Sailors' bodies, still wearing the lifejackets inscribed with the name of their boat, began washing onshore. Some of the men had their arms wrapped around each other. Some had their heads bowed over their life preservers as if in prayer. The scene was horrifying.

Identification of the ships lost at sea came mostly through the bodies. The *Wexford, Argus, McGean, Hydrus, Scott, Regina,* and *Carruthers* had all lost crew members, indicating that these vessels had foundered. At one point, a sailor with a life preserver from the *Regina* was identified as actually having been on board the *Price,* leading to great speculation as to what might have happened to the two ships. Did they collide? Was one floating on top of the other? Did the crew of one ship attempt to help the others by throwing them their life preservers? Theories were endless, but these questions remained unanswered.

Oddly, one large unidentified freighter had completely overturned, or "gone turtle" as sailors would say. No one could figure out what happened to this mystery ship. But by Saturday, November 15, the question of its identity was answered, thanks to one determined diver. Working his way around the ship in incredibly cold waters, he finally came to the hull and uncovered the ship's nameplate—*Charles S. Price,* the very ship that less than a week earlier Milton Smith had walked away from, guided by his sixth sense. He never did see his old friend Arz again. The freighter eventually sank to the bottom of Lake Huron, where it remains to this day.

The Great Lakes Storm of 1913 took the lives of 235 people, 178 in Lake Huron alone. These figures, however, are only estimates, since at the time records were not very accurate and many bodies were either never found or not identifiable. The headlines for the *Detroit News,* November 13, 1913, read: "Death Total on Lakes May Be 273." Nineteen ships, including eight massive freighters, were completely destroyed; nineteen others were left stranded.

The storm took a monumental financial toll as well. Estimates by the Carriers Association in 1913 placed the value of the ships and their more than 68 million tons of cargo at $4,782,900—or more than $105 million in today's dollars.

CLEANERS AND
DYERS WAR

1924

It was a gang war to "dye" for, quite literally. The year was 1924, and the cleaning industry in Detroit was booming. It included not only the typical mom-and-pop corner storefronts but also a gigantic collection of cleaners and dyers who serviced the wholesale market, including major clothing manufacturers and tailors. And just as in any business throughout history, owners were searching for ways to increase their profitability.

Say hello to the Purple Gang, a group of mostly Jewish mobsters led by brothers Abe, Ray, Joe, and Izzy Bernstein. No one is quite certain how they acquired their name. One theory suggests that as young boys on the streets of Detroit, they got into so much trouble that a storekeeper cried out, "These kids, they're tainted; they're rotten, purple, like the color of bad meat. They're the Purple Gang." Others thought it was because purple dye was first discovered by the Phoenicians, who originated the art of dyeing, and the gang always had a certain connection with dyers.

One thing was certain, though: In the early 1920s the Purple Gang was one of the most notorious and feared organized-crime groups anywhere. The gang was known for hijacking, gambling, arson, armed robbery, and extortion and used any type of force and violence to get their way. It's said that even Al Capone didn't want to anger them; rather than fight, he made peace with "the purples," using them as a supplier for whiskey (bootlegged through the Canadian city of Windsor) to his Chicago organization.

So when Sam Polakoff, president of the Union of Dyers and Cleaners, and Sam Sigman, secretary of Perfect Cleaners and Dyers on Caniff Avenue, decided they wanted to raise their prices from 50 cents to $1.50, with some prodding by a top Chicago racketeer, they hired the Purple Gang to "convince" their competitors to hike their cleaning fees, too. To do the cleaners' "dirty" work, the Purples were paid $1,000 a week ($13,000 in today's dollars). That's a pretty penny for a group of uneducated thugs to bring home every seven days.

What did the Purple Gang do for $1,000 a week? Essentially working as terrorists, they used every method of harassment possible to keep both union and non-union independent cleaners in line with the corrupt policies. Cleaning facilities were firebombed. Windows were smashed. Clothing was stolen. Trucks were vandalized. As notification of their presence and a warning sign, the gang would leave their "calling" card in front of an establishment: a stick of dynamite with a half-burned wick. Cleaners all over Detroit lost hundreds of thousands of dollars in property damage. For example, a stick of dynamite caused $5,000 worth of damage to the Empire Cleaners and Dyers facility. Many of those who didn't cooperate with the price hike were either beaten or mysteriously never seen again. The Cleaners and Dyers War became so intense and vicious that some in the business closed their shops and left Michigan completely.

In the end, Polakoff and Sigman themselves suffered the wrath of the Purple Gang. When Sigman decided he wanted to opt out of the arrangement, he was given a warning: His trucks were burned, and his plant was bombed. But he didn't heed the warning, and his body was later found riddled with bullets. Polakoff, too, was "taken for a ride"; his remains were discovered soon afterward in an abandoned car. The coroner's report listed the official cause of death as repeated pounding with a hammer.

After at least two years of seemingly nonstop violence within the cleaning industry, these two murders were the turning point for the Detroit police. They now believed they had the evidence needed to indict the Purple Gang in what appeared to be an open-and-shut case. At least twenty independent cleaners said they were willing to testify that they had been maliciously attacked and harassed for years.

In 1928 the highly anticipated trial began against Abe and Ray Bernstein, Eddie Fletcher, Irving Milberg, Harry Keywell, and Charles Jacoby. The courtroom was filled to capacity, and hordes of people waited in line to jam the standing-room-only section, eager to see the Purple Gang finally get what they had coming to them.

It didn't quite come out that way. Once on the stand, the prosecution's witnesses, one after another, changed their stories, or perhaps someone had "convinced" them to change their stories. When all the testimony was over, the case was sent to the jury on September 13, 1928. It took slightly more than sixty minutes for the jurors to agree on their verdict: not guilty. The underworld of crime appeared to have beaten the system again, and all the defendants were acquitted.

The cleaners and dyers may not have won the courtroom case, but the war was over. After years of price gouging, price fixing, and other underhanded tactics, the wholesale cleaners went on to resume their once "spotless" business.

Historically, the Purple Gang remains one of the lesser-known organized-crime groups, but they did manage to catch the eye of the FBI, which credits them with some five hundred unsolved murders, beating even Al Capone's body count. And the entertainment world has memorialized them in various art forms. In his popular James Bond novel *Goldfinger* (1959), author Ian Fleming created the character Helmut M. Springer, who was identified as a member of Detroit's Purple Gang. Two years later, Hollywood produced a black-and-white movie entitled *The Purple Gang,* starring Barry Sullivan and Robert Blake. Finally, the King himself, Elvis Presley, sang about them in his 1957 hit "Jailhouse Rock," crediting the musical force of the inmates' rhythm section to the colorful Purple Gang.

THE OSSIAN SWEET TRIAL

1925

Ossian Sweet was a medical doctor, specializing in gynecology, when he left his home state of Florida to settle in the manufacturing boomtown of Detroit. Life was good until 1925, when the African American doctor decided to move his wife and infant daughter into a two-story bungalow in an all-white neighborhood. Because of that relocation and a series of ill-fated events, Dr. Sweet would soon find himself on trial for murder.

Although Detroit at this time had 80,000 black residents, it was very much a segregated city. The Ku Klux Klan (KKK), targeting blacks and Catholic and Jewish immigrants, had an even greater presence, with some 100,000 members living in the city. In 1924 a Ku Klux Klansman ran for mayor, actually winning the majority of votes. However, because he was a write-in candidate, election officials refused to verify his votes since his name had been written with numerous misspellings.

The influx of newly transplanted workers created a serious housing problem, especially for blacks who were crammed into a couple of east-side areas known as Black Bottom and Paradise Valley, an area that was anything but what the name implies. Several families often had to live together in a single flat, longing to escape their residential confinement.

Like many other blacks, Dr. Ossian Sweet hoped to improve his family's living conditions. His successful career afforded him the ability to make a $3,500 nonrefundable down payment on an $18,500 house on Garland Street, also on the east side, but in an all-white neighborhood. The minute he signed the purchase agreement, word got out that a black family was moving into a white neighborhood.

His new neighbors were not happy. They immediately formed a cohesive block club to prevent the Sweets from moving in.

And Sweet was ready for them. Determined not to be bullied, he told his friends that his family wasn't looking for any trouble, but if any trouble arose, they would be prepared to protect themselves.

The day, September 8, was unseasonably warm when the family nervously drove to their new home. The Detroit police had been called in to stand guard just in case anyone got out of line. Yet all was quiet and peaceful during the move.

Not much furniture was carried in, but there was the all-important gunnysack, which Ossian personally handled. Inside he had hidden his family's safeguard: a shotgun, two rifles, six revolvers, and four hundred rounds of ammunition. As evening fell, people congregated on the street outside the house, but there was no violence. Still, Dr. Sweet felt uneasy, and the next night he invited more of his friends and family to stay with him. Inside the home now were his brothers Otis and Henry; his college roommate, John Latting; Joe Mack, their chauffeur; Norris Murray, a handyman; Edna Butler and Serena Rochelle, both friends of Gladys Sweet, Ossian's wife; and William Davis, a federal narcotics agent.

The calm of the previous night was replaced by larger, angrier crowds, shouting and pelting the house with stones. Fearful, the men inside took up arms. Ossian cried out, "They're ruining my property." And with that, shots rang out from the second-story window. One of those shots killed Leon Breiner, who was standing on his porch across the street. Another neighbor, Eric Hougberg, took a bullet in his thigh.

Within seconds, the police rushed the Sweet house and arrested everyone inside, charging them all with murder. Authorities quickly decided to hold all of them without bail. The National Association for the Advancement of Colored People immediately got involved, determined to get the best defense attorney possible. Their top choice was Clarence Darrow, who had studied at the University of Michigan Law School and just months before had gained notoriety as the defense attorney in the Scopes "monkey trial."

At sixty-nine years of age, Darrow wasn't looking for more high-profile cases, yet he agreed to defend Sweet when he heard that one of the people in Sweet's house had indeed fired the shot. "I'll take the case," he said. "If they had not had the courage to shoot back in defense of their own lives, I wouldn't think they were worth defending."

Jury selection was exhausting, and it took days to seat the twelve jurors, all white males. The trial, which began on November 5, was assigned to Judge Frank Murphy, a highly respected public servant. The courtroom was standing room only.

Eyewitnesses gave widely conflicting testimony, including how many people were in the crowd around Sweet's house. The prosecutor's witnesses vowed there were never more than thirty. Police said it was a small crowd, around fifteen. A *Detroit News* reporter stated that the crowd he saw was "between four hundred and five hundred people," many of them throwing stones against the house "like hail."

Some of the most powerful testimony came from a witness who was standing next to Leon Breiner when he was killed. Asked what Breiner had in his hand, the witness responded that he was holding a pipe. This statement confirmed that at the time of the murder, Breiner was not throwing stones but was innocently standing on his porch smoking.

Darrow was not to be deterred. He made the brave move of putting Ossian Sweet on the stand. He described the incidents as they unfolded. Then Darrow asked the pivotal question: "What was your state of mind at the time of the shooting?"

Ossian replied, "When I opened the door and saw the mob, I realized I was facing the same mob that had hounded my people through its entire history. In my mind I was pretty confident of what I was up against. I had my back against the wall. I was filled with a peculiar fear, the fear of one who knows the history of my race."

And with those words, the four-week trial was over.

The jury deliberated for forty-six hours but remained hopelessly deadlocked, necessitating a retrial. But this time Darrow chose a different strategy. Instead of trying all the defendants together, he opted to have them tried individually, beginning with Ossian's twenty-one-year-old brother, Henry. Nothing of consequence changed in any of the testimony. Ossian again took the stand while his brother chose to remain silent.

When it was Darrow's turn for his closing remarks, he was at the top of his game. For more than six hours, his flamboyant style alternated with soft tenderness. He spoke at times in a loud, commanding voice, followed by a subdued undertone. After recounting the horrors of slavery and the lynchings of African Americans in the South, Darrow said: "Now that is their history. . . . I believe the life of a Negro has been a life full of tragedy, of injustice, of oppression. The law had made him equal—but man has not. . . . I know that before him there is suffering, tribulation and death among the blacks, and perhaps among the whites. . . . On behalf of this defendant, on behalf of these helpless ones who turn to you . . . I ask you in the name of progress and the human race to return a verdict of not guilty in this case."

After just four hours, the jury followed his advice and returned a verdict of not guilty.

Tears streamed down the face of Henry Sweet while Ossian sat in the back, unnoticed, allowing his head to fall into his hands. Charges against all the others were dropped.

The case, with its victorious outcome for the rights of property owners, remains one of the most important cases in the history of civil rights.

DRAMATIC RESCUE AT
THE PABST MINE

1926

When the Upper Peninsula was finally recognized as being a mineral-rich land of opportunity, a flood of immigrants, most of them Finnish or Croatian, began arriving. Work was plentiful, arduous, and not without a high level of risk. The men who daily were submerged into the Pabst iron ore mine were constantly aware of the extraordinary challenges they faced. Yet no one could ever have predicted the accident in 1926 that left forty-three miners in a battle for their lives.

September that year had atypical weather. Instead of the usual sunny skies, a foreboding series of clouds inundated the area with rain. The deluge forced the cancellation of school football games and the Gogebic county fair, as well as the suspension of ongoing farming and building projects. Flooding made roads impassable. An estimated eleven inches of rain fell between September 22 and 24, and forecasts called for more of the same, and maybe even some snow.

The wet weather made travel difficult, but many of the miners at Pabst lived close enough to walk. On September 24, determined to collect their $4-a-day wage, forty-six men trekked through water-logged Ironwood to enter the mine's "G" shaft.

Entering the mine was a laborious task. This relatively new, yet highly productive shaft was just 10 feet by a little over 18 feet, dug on a 64-degree incline. An elevator lowered the men almost 2,600 feet, moving at a top speed of 1,000 feet per minute.

For three electricians, the ride down that Friday became their last, as one of the cables broke, causing the elevator to fall uncontrollably to the bottom. Rocks and boulders tumbled down, completely sealing off the shaft and leaving the forty-three other men trapped inside the darkness.

At first, the men were staggered between three levels, but they wearily managed to congregate on the eighth level, about eight hundred feet underground. Unable to hear anything from the outside world, they began to wonder. How long would they be there? What was happening around them? Would more rocks come tumbling down? How would they manage to stay alive?

Because the men didn't know how long they would be trapped underground, they decided to ration whatever food they had with them. Sandwiches were eaten a half inch at a time. After the second day, their provisions were gone, but their resourcefulness was not. They turned to the wooden planks on the mine's walls, scraped the birch bark off with their fingernails, and heated it with their carbide lamps to create their own brand of "tree tea," their last remaining form of nourishment.

The days came and went. To help pass the time, the group talked about life and politics, sang hymns, and prayed, offering hope and consolation to those whose faith and strength were waning.

In the meantime, crews had been drilling through the rock in an adjacent shaft, where they were able to go down 2,400 feet to a tunnel crossing between the H and G shafts. On day five, at nine o'clock at night, after 129 hours of quiet skepticism and entombment, Thomas Trewarth heard the familiar voice of George Hawes. Instantaneously he cried out to the others, "Yoho—boys—wake up—they're here."

Unsteady and weak, yet filled with excitement, the men knew that their ordeal would soon be over. The team of rescuers became physical support to all those stranded men, who tediously had to backtrack, going down another 1,600 feet before crossing through to the next shaft to reclaim their freedom. At 9:22 p.m. the door of the H shaft swung open, releasing first Samuel F. Sinkelma to a thunderous roar from 7,000 anxious supporters. One by one, all forty-three returned to safety.

When the men were asked what they wanted most, they unanimously answered, "Tobacco." Hawes happened to have a cigar with him, which was passed around like a peace pipe, each man taking a comforting puff.

Relieved family and friends embraced their loved ones, and then the long-awaited celebration of gratitude began, continuing for hours. Musicians played, people danced, and all of Ironwood "went wild with joy." Eventually the police were called in to maintain some semblance of peace.

"Bearded, haggard, and wrapped in blankets," the newly released men responded to inquiries about how they had survived with so little food: "It wasn't bad, you get sick from hunger after the first day or so and then it doesn't bother you. We didn't dare think of food, however." When asked what they talked about, they responded "It made us feel better to pray." And what about work? "Yes, we will be back at work in a couple of days." Then they were whisked to the Grandview Hospital, where they were treated with lots of food and plenty of tender, loving care.

Afterward, a finger of blame was pointed at Michael Collins, who had been the county mining inspector at the time of the accident.

His responsibilities included a thorough examination of the shaft, which had been previously cited for safety violations. The towns-people faulted him, saying that much-needed repairs were never made. They went so far as to physically threaten him. His son stood guard protectively, on the front porch of his home, accompanied by his deer hunting rifle. Had Collins's negligence caused the accident? Or had all the rain that fell into the shaft weakened the structure and perhaps caused the rocks to crack as they froze and thawed? No one will ever know for certain.

What is certain is that the successful rescue in 1926 will likely remain one of the most dramatic rescues of all time. The story made headlines in almost every newspaper across the country. And yes, the men were true to their word. Within just a few days of their recovery, they were all back on the job, continuing to extract the iron ore.

BATH SCHOOL DISASTER

1927

The morning of Wednesday, May 18, 1927, in Bath started out like any other spring morning. There had been an electrical storm the night before, typical for that time of year. School was coming to a close in just a couple of days, and children were anxiously awaiting their summer break. Some of the youngsters reluctantly got ready for the school day, while others excitedly raced to Bath's newly consolidated school, which now housed all students from elementary through high school. The consolidation was a welcome change to most, as siblings and friends could now remain together in one school. Life seemed pleasantly normal in every way.

One of those unhappy with the consolidation was Andrew Kehoe, elected treasurer of the school board. He had voted against the plan; he was outraged because he felt that taxes in the small town were already far too high. Born in 1872 in Tecumseh, Keho was one of thirteen children. Over the years his life had taken some unfortunate turns. Behind closed doors, rumors swirled that he had been responsible for his stepmother being burned to death. After he was married, he had an accident that left him in a coma for weeks. And in Bath, his financial troubles were rapidly mounting, with the threat of foreclosure on his farm.

One bright spot for Kehoe was his talent and passion for electricity. At a young age he became fascinated with all things electrical and is believed to have studied electrical engineering at both Michigan State College (now Michigan State University) and a school in St. Louis, Missouri.

With his various technical skills, it was a natural fit for Kehoe to become a handyman at the Bath school, and he was hired in the later part of 1926. He also needed the money.

Unfortunately, his intentions were not to do maintenance at the school, but secretly to get revenge on children for the increasing school taxes that he believed were the cause of all his money woes.

As Kehoe's wife, Nellie, was rapidly becoming more ill, he was seen spending more and more time at the school. That was after he had spent weeks buying crates from a number of different stores in Lansing, most of them labeled with three simple words: "High Explosives. Dangerous." Inside the school, he laid thousands of feet of electrical wiring, creating an extremely detailed system, and then hid his recently purchased dynamite in the basement. During that same time, he was also setting explosives around his own property, which was still in dire financial straits.

On that seemingly peaceful, sunny morning of May 18, as the classrooms filled with students, Kehoe was seen nervously going in and out of the school several times, appearing to move at an almost frantic pace. Then he drove away. Just minutes later, around 8:45 a.m., Kehoe's preset timer in the school went off; electricity shot through the wires that he had meticulously laid, detonating the explosives; and minutes later a powerful blast occurred in the north wing of the building. The walls appeared to lift right to the sky and then came thunderously crashing to the ground in a pile of rubble, causing the roof to collapse. After a split second of silence, the deafening, high-pitched screams began. The crumbled school resembled a horrific war zone. People were flung out of broken windows. Blood-stained bodies were strewn everywhere.

The explosion was heard and felt throughout the entire neighborhood, with many thinking an earthquake had struck. Windows had been demolished in nearby homes. Instantly people ran out to see what had happened, and soon there were many cries of "the school has been blown up." People charged to the scene of the crime, hysterically searching for their loved ones.

In the midst of the bedlam, Kehoe amazingly returned to the school in his junk-filled truck and noticed the school superintendent, Emory E. Huyck, among those working tirelessly to save anyone from the carnage. Kehoe, who had never been especially fond of Huyck, called him over to his vehicle. As Huyck approached, Kehoe took a gun and shot at the apparent junk in the backseat. The dynamite, hidden underneath, instantly exploded, dismembering the bodies of both Kehoe and Huyck. That second detonation also killed the local postmaster, a retired farmer, and Cleo Clayton, an eight-year-old student who had managed to survive the blast at the school but was unable to escape the deadly flying shrapnel this time.

When the Michigan State Police arrived on the scene, they put a temporary halt to the all-consuming rescue efforts. They wanted to be 100 percent certain that no other explosives were hidden on the grounds. Once inside, they quickly learned that Kehoe's electrical skills were less than perfect, since only half of his plan had actually been executed. In the basement, the police were shocked to find more than five hundred pounds of dynamite that had never ignited.

In the midst of all the gruesome chaos, little attention was paid to the burst of flames shooting out of the farmhouse that belonged to Andrew Kehoe. His plan to burn down his house worked too, destroying his home, all the farm animals, and his sick wife, who was trapped inside. Left behind, on the surrounding picket fence, were the ominous words that Kehoe had hand-stenciled: "Criminals are made, not born."

The devastation was so immense that the Bath town hall was set up as a morgue for the bodies of thirty-six children and two teachers. One of them was twenty-one-year-old Hazel Weatherby, who was found cradling two of her young students in her arms. Ten-year-old Beatrice Gibbs clung to life until August 23.

When it was all over, thirty-eight children and seven adults were dead (including the murderer Andrew Kehoe and his wife). Another fifty-eight children and adults had been seriously injured, making the Bath school tragedy the largest school disaster anywhere in America.

Afterward, the people of Bath gathered their faith and pulled together, living in the hope of the future, and focused their attention on building a new school. On August 18, 1928, the new James Couzens Agricultural School was dedicated to its "living youth."

Today, on the site of the old school is the James Couzens Memorial Park (named after the state senator who donated funds to help build the new school), where a plaque was erected listing all the names of those killed, except the two Kehoes, whose names were purposely omitted. In the center of the park stands an old wooden tower, the original cupola from the Bath Consolidated School. In 1992 the State of Michigan placed a historical maker there, telling the never-to-be-forgotten fatal story.

It's a story of incomprehensible sadness, a story that ironically began with an electrical storm and ended with one that no one could have ever imagined. All because of one man's overwhelming and twisted desire for revenge.

BATTLE OF THE OVERPASS

1937

It was almost time for the three o'clock shift change at the Ford Rouge Plant in Dearborn, where 9,000 employees would be crossing over the Miller Road at Gate 4. If you had a message you wanted to get out to as many of the workers as possible, this was the optimum opportunity. On this Wednesday afternoon, May 26, 1937, union organizers had an innocent plan to reach the workers by having auxiliary women hand out "Unionism, not Fordism" pamphlets. No one was prepared for the resistance they were about to meet.

Labor struggles were nothing new, especially in the auto industry. Just two years before, Congress had passed the National Labor Relations Act, giving workers the right to collective bargaining, with the intent to stop unscrupulous activity on both sides. The United Auto Workers (UAW) had set their sights on Ford Motor Company, which so far had shown the most resistance to unionization of the Big Three automakers. Founding father Henry Ford was vehemently opposed to giving up any control of his groundbreaking manufacturing system.

Viewing all the Rouge workers as potential members, the union decided to reach out to them. It rented two nearby vacant buildings and set up headquarters. The union obtained a license to distribute its literature from the city of Dearborn. The message inside was clear: Raise the rate of pay from $6 a day to $8. That was more than a 33 percent increase, substantial by anyone's standards and better than the competitors' pay.

To maximize exposure, the union alerted media outlets, attracting crowds of curious onlookers and newshounds. The stage was carefully set. The main players—chief union organizer Richard Truman Frankensteen, president of UAW Local 174; Walter Reuther; and several of their colleagues—were ready to make their grand entrance. Around 2:00 p.m., smiling confidently, they began their march up the stairs to the pedestrian overpass. The camera of *Detroit News* photographer James E. (Scotty) Kilpatrick started clicking away as an anonymous shout rang out: "You're on Ford property. Get the hell off here!"

Unbeknownst to the union team, Henry Bennett, head of Ford security, had assembled more than thirty of his "service men" to ward off potential trouble. Before anyone could react to the order to leave, several rugged men pounced on Frankensteen, pulled his coat over his head, and started punching and kicking him incessantly. Frankensteen was a physically powerful man himself, having played football at the University of Dayton. His attackers, clearly outnumbering him, were not deterred and persisted in pummeling their victim until he fell to the ground.

Simultaneously, the auxiliary women were pushed and shoved, and Reuther, too, in his words, "was punched and kicked and dragged by my feet to the stairway, thrown down the first flight of steps, picked up, slammed down on the platform and kicked down the second flight." Watching this violent scene, Dearborn police turned their heads the other way. Kilpatrick's camera, however, captured images of every action.

As soon as the company thugs realized that their images were being caught on film, they switched gears and made a beeline for the photographer. Filled with adrenaline, Kilpatrick sprinted in escape to his car. Instantly, he ripped out the photo plates, hid them under his backseat, and loaded his camera with blank ones.

The service men pounded repeatedly on his window, demanding the film. Finally, Kilpatrick relented and sheepishly opened his camera, handing over the contents. It wasn't until the next morning, when the photos of the bloodied Reuther and Frankensteen made front-page news, that they learned they had been duped.

The aftermath of the incident took its toll on Ford, creating a public relations nightmare.

News outlets across the country carried a detailed description of the brutality used on Frankensteen, who gave a detailed account to the *Communist Daily Worker:*

> *They knocked me down again, turned me over on my side and began to kick me in the stomach. When I would protect my side they would kick my head. One of the attackers would say, "That is enough. Let him go." Then they would pick me up and stand me on my feet, but I was no sooner on my feet than they would knock me down again. This went on about five times. They let me lie there for a while. . . . Every once in a while someone would grind his heel into me. . . . It was the worst licking I've ever taken.*

Reports continued to flood the media about injuries to other union men. Robert Kanter had been pushed off the bridge, falling thirty feet. Richard Merriweather had his back broken. Numerous others were critically wounded.

As the overseer of it all, Henry Bennett felt obliged to issue a statement in an attempt to protect his employer and his reputation. In his own defense, he told *Time* magazine: "The affair was deliberately provoked by union officials . . . they simply wanted to trump up a charge of Ford Brutality. . . . I know definitely no Ford service man or plant police were involved in any way in the fight. . . . The union men were beaten by regular Ford employees who were on their way to work. The union men called them 'scabs and cursed and taunted them.'"

Too little, too late. His words didn't resonate with anyone. Public sympathy had clearly swayed in favor of the union. The National Labor Relations Board investigated the incident and found Ford in violation of the relatively new law. The company was told that it must immediately stop getting in the way of any attempts at unionizing its workforce.

Henry Ford's disappointment was more than a business defeat. His prized Rouge plant, patterned after his own residential estate, was purposely gated, fenced, and guarded, with no direct access to public streets. Yet all the preventative security had failed to thwart this horrific scene.

What came to be known as the infamous "Battle of the Overpass" was the beginning of the end of Ford Motor's existence as a free shop. In 1941 the company signed a contract of agreement with the United Auto Workers union.

DETROIT RACE RIOTS

1943

Race riots in Detroit were nothing new. The first one dated as far back as 1833, four years before Michigan even became a state. Slave hunters made the journey north to reclaim a couple who had escaped via the Underground Railroad. A local court ruled that the husband and wife were rightfully the property of their "owner," a decision that ignited an outbreak of fighting between blacks and whites, resulting in deaths and mounting hostilities.

In some ways, the Detroit riots of 1943 may have been a carryover of that initial turmoil. Uneasiness existed here for a number of reasons. The country was in the midst of World War II, which added pressure on the city to manufacture war goods. More workers were needed for the factories, and recruiters headed south in search of employees willing to put in forty-eight-hour workweeks. The number of blacks in the United States' fourth-largest city rapidly grew to 200,000, a figure that caused serious housing and transportation problems. Food and gasoline were being rationed to sustain what was known as the "Arsenal of Democracy." The rest of the country was well aware of the escalating tensions. In August 1942 *Life* magazine ran a feature story focusing on the problems, called "Detroit Is Dynamite."

Ten months later, the fire was beginning to kindle. At a Packard plant, which produced engines for bombers and PT boats, 20,000 workers walked out to protest the promotion of three black workers.

On Sunday, June 20, a steamy, 90-degree day at Detroit's Belle Isle Park, the explosives really went off. Roughly 100,000 people crowded the lush island seeking recreation and some respite from their daily routine. However, that wasn't all that two young African American men had on their minds. Five days earlier, during a confrontation, they had been thrown out of the Eastwood Amusement Park. On this day, they were bent on getting their revenge.

Around ten o'clock, when the skies had just grown dark, the two ruffians went into action, slugging a white pedestrian crossing the bridge. Instantly, others came to his defense. Soon, more than two hundred men, women, and children were involved in a black and white brawl. On the scene, police began to search cars entering or leaving the island, but only those carrying black passengers. Vehicles belonging to whites were not inspected. Just after midnight, things started to calm down. The still-irritable crowds dispersed, with blacks and whites going their separate ways.

The African Americans congregated at the Forest Club, a popular nightclub in a dismal section of town ironically called Paradise Valley. Drinks were being gulped down fast and furiously when Charles (Little Willie) Lyons and Leo Tipton stood up in front of the crowd, grabbed a microphone, and announced, falsely, that some white folks had just thrown an African American woman and her baby over the Belle Isle Bridge, killing them both.

That one false statement detonated an explosion the likes of which Detroit had never seen. A frenzied mob of five hundred filled the streets, looted white-owned stores along Hastings Street, threw bricks at the windows of passing motorists, and attacked every white person they saw. Streetcars were stopped, and whites were pulled off and stoned. Parked cars were overturned.

As if the fire needed any more fuel, not far away, a group of southern whites started their own rumor—that African Americans had raped a white woman on the same bridge, causing her to fall to her death into the Detroit River. African American now became the target of almost barbaric violence. As they left all-night movie theaters, they were hit and dragged through the streets. Their cars were torched. Some even reported that they were assaulted with tear gas.

By 4:00 a.m., the white mob had grown to more than 250 and showed no signs of stopping their attacks. The police, who were grossly outnumbered, were ordered to shoot to kill all looters who didn't follow orders. The oldest paved street in the state, Woodward Avenue, became a racial dividing line. Onlookers, 100,000 strong, filled Grand Circus Park. This volcanic eruption showed no signs of slowing down.

Sixteen hours into the fighting, Detroit Mayor Edward Jeffries Jr. realized that the situation was far too big for the city to handle, and he urged Governor Harry Kelly to take some drastic measures. Kelly contacted President Franklin D. Roosevelt and begged him for national assistance.

One thousand federal troops arrived at 11:00 p.m. on June 21, just a little over twenty-four hours after the first punch was thrown. The big guns rolled into town, literally. Jeeps and vehicles armed with rifles and machine guns wheeled down the streets. And the citizens took heed, one by one slowly dispersing. The city appeared to be back in control.

The statistics for the melee are startling. Officially, the death toll was recorded at thirty-four, twenty-five of them African American. Seventeen of the African American fatalities were the result of police bullets. Almost seven hundred more were injured, 1,800 were arrested, and $2 million of property was destroyed. Factories had to be shut down, causing another $1 million in lost war production. The Detroit race riot even got a reaction out of Adolf Hitler, who commented through the German-controlled Vichy radio that the riot was an example of "the internal disorganization of a country torn by social injustice, race hatreds, regional disputes, the violence of an irritated proletariat, and the gangsterism of a capitalistic police." The city's all-white police force faced a lot of criticism for their prejudicial treatment of African Americans, and soon afterward, recruiting began for two hundred black police officers.

You may be wondering what happened to Tipton and Lyons, the pair who voiced the initial lie. They were sentenced to two to five years in prison for inciting a riot—a riot that would leave a scar on the history of Detroit forever.

JAPANESE BALLOON BOMBS

1945

Everyone in 1945 was talking about the devastation of World War II and the huge loss of lives around the globe. Americans suffered nearly 400,000 deaths and a million casualties, although most citizens believed they had been spared from actual combat on U.S. soil. Those at home didn't really worry that the enemy would attack them in their own backyard—that is, until some unsuspecting Michigan residents discovered the war's best-kept secret.

On a mid-winter Friday afternoon, February 23, 1945, three young boys in North Dorr were heading home from school, excited about the upcoming weekend. Kicking their way home through rural fields, Larry Bailey and brothers Kenneth and Robert Fein noticed something eerily unfamiliar floating in the sky. Could it be a bird? No. Perhaps a kite? No, not that either. As it fell closer to earth, they identified it as a very large balloon with nineteen strong ropes attached.

Since the balloon was so cumbersome, the trio summoned a neighbor, Joe Wolk, to help them remove their finding from 146th Avenue and 21st Street and take it to the Feins' home. There, Mrs.

Marguerite Fein was visiting with the family priest, Father Ernest Walters, who took one look at the peculiar balloon and suggested that she contact the Kent County sheriff. At first the sheriff thought it was a type of weather balloon, but that notion proved incorrect. At a loss for proper identification, Deputies Al Renis and George Laman called the FBI. Within twenty-four hours, the balloon was on its way to the Naval Technical Air Intelligence Center at Anacostia, in the District of Columbia.

The buzz throughout the normally calm North Allegan County community quickly centered on the mysterious balloon. Everyone was whispering about the strange mass that had fallen out of the sky. Local newspaper reporters were chomping at the bit to get behind the real story. Yet the FBI and all military personnel remained vigilantly tight-lipped. What could possibly cause the authorities to be so secretive?

The saga of the mysterious balloon added another chapter on Sunday, March 25, when, several hundred miles away in Farmington, Michigan, loud popping sounds were heard, followed by an unexplained fire on vacant property at 20951 Gill Road. Assuming that children had built a bonfire, neighbors didn't give the incident much thought at the time. The next month, however, John T. Cook, who lived next door, was working in his garden when he unearthed a shiny tin can. Not thinking much of that either, he tossed it aside.

But this is where the constant investigative work by reporters began to pull the whole story together. On June 6 a short newspaper article was written about the quirky Japanese balloon bomb, an experimental weapon used by the Japanese during World War II. The military was inundated with so many questions that it was forced to issue an official statement about the bombs' existence.

The Japanese had, indeed, masterminded hydrogen balloons, made of paper or silk, measuring about 33 feet in diameter and capable of lifting around 1,000 pounds. They were equipped with varying loads, from a 26-pound incendiary device to one 33-pound antipersonnel bomb with four 11-pound incendiary devices attached. More than 9,200 of these hot-air balloon weapons were launched from the Japanese island of Honshu between November 3, 1944, and mid-April 1945. The Japanese plan was as follows: The balloons would catch a ride on the jet stream, soar across the ocean, and land on the West Coast of the United States, where the forests were thick and lush. Then, when they hit the ground, their explosive power would wreak havoc, and the massive fires they caused would be so widely publicized that every American would know the Japanese had hit their mark.

There are two reasons that this plan never materialized. First, U.S. authorities, well aware of the existence of the balloon bombs, took every precautionary measure to make sure that no media outlet leaked a word to the public. On January, 4, 1945, the U.S. Office of Censorship issued a statement asking every form of broadcast or print media to adopt a code of silence so as not to cause any panic with the public. It may have been difficult for journalists not to reveal the story, yet they respected the ban and kept the story of the balloons secret for months.

Second, of the more than 9,000 balloons that were deployed, only about 300 of them were known to have hit ground. Most of them were found in areas of northern California, Washington state, and Oregon. On May 5, 1945, when a woman and five children were having a picnic in Bly, Oregon, they noticed one of the balloons in the woods. They attempted to drag it out, but sadly, all six were killed when it exploded. That incident resulted in the only fatalities from these unusual weapons and also forced the government to issue a statement warning people not to touch them. A simple description and very limited information were released, since no one really knew where they might have landed. The bombs were said to have traveled as far as Canada, Mexico, and, surprisingly, Michigan.

After Farmington's John T. Cook read about the balloon bomb in June 1945, he revisited the now-rusted tin can he had found earlier. He called over his neighbor, Michigan State Police Sergeant William Hedt, and asked him to take a look at it. They both agreed that it looked similar to the description of the bomb in the newspaper, so they turned it over to authorities, who confirmed that it was an incendiary canister from a Japanese balloon bomb. And the popping noise, followed by the "bonfire," was actually the effect of the bomb in action. It is believed that the bomb had traveled more than 6,000 miles, making the Farmington site the easternmost destination of any of the bombs launched.

When the war ended, the media censorship ban was lifted, but by that time people had turned their attention to other topics, leaving the Japanese balloon bombs unknown to many Americans even today. Those with knowledge of them occasionally would let their imaginations run wild. It was reported that someone in Sault Ste. Marie thought they saw one in the sky, but it turned out to be the planet Venus. Across the country, another creative mind also thought they saw a balloon bomb overhead, so they took a gun and shot at it. Apparently, there are now a few bullet holes in a certain Nebraska water tower.

LOST IN SPACE: NW FLIGHT 2501

1950

The world of aviation was still in its youthful stage when the DC-4 was first developed. The DC-4 was an innovative airliner for its time, and the U.S. Army drafted it into service in February 1942, following the bombing of Pearl Harbor. Although the planes were strong and sturdy, the end of World War II left them as orphans without a home. Instead of mothballing them, the military sold them to commercial airlines for a mere $90,000. Originally having a forty-person capacity, they were converted to a crammed sixty-seat passenger plane. The cabin was unpressurized, restricting the aircraft to low and potentially turbulent altitudes. But the planes had survived the war, so it seemed impossible that they couldn't weather a Michigan storm.

On Friday, June 23, 1950, people waited patiently in LaGuardia airport, anticipating their lengthy flight to Seattle with routine stops in Minneapolis, Minnesota, and Spokane, Washington. Northwest Flight 2501 was booked to its sixty person capacity. Boarding went smoothly. The group of enthusiastic travelers, a few with butterflies in their stomachs, took their assigned seats in preparation for takeoff.

As the flight attendant conducted her head count, she discovered that five reserved passengers were missing. There were schedules to keep, so even though they had purchased tickets, they would just be out of luck, and the flight would go on without them.

In New York, it was a pleasant summer evening, enabling the DC-4 to lift off on time at 7:31 p.m. It was carrying fifty-five passengers, a pilot, a copilot, one flight attendant, 2,500 gallons of fuel, 8 gallons of oil, and 490 pounds of express freight. In total, that accounted for 71,342 pounds, only 58 pounds below the maximum allowed for takeoff.

As the aircraft began its ascent, travelers peered through the windows at crystal-clear skies. However, activity in the cockpit wasn't that relaxed. Pilot Robert C. Lind, who had been flying a DC-4 continuously for the past five years, was uneasy about his flight plan, which included cruising at 6,000 feet. Pending thunderstorms en route caused him originally to ask to fly at 4,000 feet, but the Air Route Traffic Control (ARTC) denied his request, saying that that level had already been assigned to other planes.

A little more than two hours into the flight, which was now over Cleveland, Ohio, Lind again pleaded for a lower altitude. This time the ARTC agreed to 4,000 feet. But just forty minutes later, the flight was ordered to drop even lower, to 3,500 feet. Severe storms over Lake Michigan were making it difficult for an eastbound flight to maintain its altitude of 5,000 feet, and it was necessary to maintain a significant distance between the two.

Weather in Michigan that night was so ferocious that three pilots from the Detroit airport had earlier decided to turn around and return safely to the gate. Forceful turbulence was prevalent as Flight 2501 crossed over Battle Creek, necessitating another call at 11:13 p.m. for yet another drop in altitude. This request was denied. Lind acknowledged reception of the information at 11:15 p.m.

Not until 11:37 p.m. did the ARTC realize that the flight was now ten minutes overdue. All nearby airports frantically attempted to establish communications, but to no avail. Captain Lind's voice was never to be heard again. At 5:30 the next morning, it was presumed that there had been some type of accident. The plane did not have enough fuel to sustain flight for that length of time.

What could have possibly caused the plane to drop out of the sky? Was it a midair explosion? Or something else? The more wreckage authorities could uncover, the greater their chances of solving the mystery.

The official investigation began at sunrise on the morning of Saturday, June 24, the day before the outbreak of the Korean War. After many long, tedious hours, a Coast Guard cutter informed the Civil Aeronautics Board that they had found "an oil slick, aircraft debris, and the aircraft log book in Lake Michigan approximately eighteen miles north-northwest of Benton Harbor."

Coast Guard experts theorized that high winds may have "twisted" the plane, causing it to expel sparks, possibly starting a major fire in the fuel tank. But that hypothesis was soon proven to be false.

As search efforts continued, only floating debris was recovered: foam rubber seat cushions, pillows, arm rests, a fuel tank float, blankets, pieces of clothing, and luggage. The coarsely shredded condition of the cushions and pillows suggested that at the time of impact the flight was traveling at a high speed. Rather than something unusual happening midair, it was more probable that the plane was fully intact when it hit the water. Substantial pieces of debris were never located. Small pieces eventually washed ashore, including scattered human body parts. Coast Guard Captain Nathaniel Fulford confirmed that the biggest piece of wreckage was "no bigger than your hand." Beaches in nearby South Haven remained closed for nearly two weeks while crews continued their detective work.

Gone forever were fifty-eight people: twenty-eight women, twenty-four men, and six children, none of them from Michigan. The Kokanson family had all been traveling together: John and Kay, with their seven-year-old daughter, Janice, and their four-year-old son, Thomas. William Freng, vice president of International Telephone and Telegraph Corporation, was traveling with his wife, Rosa, and their eighteen-year-old daughter, Barbara.

Eventually a few belongings from other passengers began to tell more personal stories. For example, papers inside the wallet of Frank Schwartz revealed that he was on his way to fulfill his duties as father of the bride at his daughter's wedding in St. Paul, Minnesota.

Several witnesses testified at Civil Aeronautic Board hearings in Chicago. One claimed that at about 12:20 a.m. on Saturday he had heard the plane flying over his home. In his testimony to the CAB, one man stated, "I took a look out of the window and he seemed to be flying pretty low. . . . Minutes later, there was a terrific flash out in the lake." Another man said he was sitting outside his gas station at 12:15 a.m. when he saw the plane overhead and heard its motors "plunk twice followed by a queer flash of light." Still, no definitive explanations were ever produced, and official records bluntly list the plane as "written off."

For years divers and researchers have attempted to find any significant pieces of the plane, hoping to bring together the pieces of this puzzle. Author Clive Cussler, as head of the National Underwater and Marine Agency, has made it his mission to help solve this continuing mystery.

Holland-based Valerie van Heest of the Michigan Shipwreck Research Association made her own unusual discovery in St. Joseph's Riverview Cemetery. She learned that the bodies that had washed ashore were buried in a mass unmarked grave. Apparently, the coroner took whatever remains had been found as of July 1, 1950, and

buried them in a city-donated plot, never notifying any of the families. In September 2008 van Heest gathered the family members of
the deceased for an official burial and the placement of a forty-inch
granite memorial headstone.

While there may never be an answer for the greatest air disaster
of its time, at least now there may be some comforting peace for the
victims' families.

BRIDGING THE GAP

1957

Visionaries in Michigan have been pursuing the idea of bridging the state's two peninsulas together since 1883, the year the Brooklyn Bridge was completed. Faced with a challenging hurdle, they began a subtle campaign. The next year, a St. Ignace store owner, hoping to implant a subliminal message, put a picture of the Brooklyn Bridge on his shopping bags, superimposing the state's emblem over it, with the words, "A Glimpse of the Future—Proposed Bridge across the Straits of Michigan."

In reality, there was no proposed bridge. But its necessity grew more apparent. Taking promoters of the bridge another step closer was the Grand Hotel on Mackinac Island. The hotel was built in 1887 by high-powered railroad financiers, but the board of directors soon became frustrated with their investment. Chairman Cornelius Vanderbilt garnered some attention when he forcefully stated that they now had the largest hotel of its kind in the world for a very short business season. What they really needed was a bridge to bring people across the Straits. Planting another seed in 1920 was the state's first highway commissioner, Horatio "Good Roads" Earle, who imagined a "floating tunnel."

Soon afterward, a car ferry service was instituted. It operated almost 365 days a year by using ice cutters in the winter, but although it hauled 9,000 vehicles a day, it couldn't meet the escalating demand. As years went by, especially during deer-hunting season, the wait to ferry across the Straits could be as long as nineteen hours.

An intense game of political ping-pong went on for decades. One party of politicians would be in favor of a permanent crossway, while the other would be opposed. Then their positions would flip the other way. In this sea of dreams, questions were repeatedly asked: "If we build it, will they cross? How will we pay for it? Can the underlying rocks sustain a bridge of that magnitude?" The naysayers' voices were always louder than those of the bridge's enthusiasts. Agreement on anything seemed to be impossible. Then World War II started, halting any further talk about a bridge.

In 1950 Governor G. Mennen "Soapy" Williams rekindled the flame by establishing the Mackinac Bridge Authority to study every angle of feasibility. After exhaustive and expensive research, the Bridge Authority members concluded: "It can be done. Let's do it." They determined that the needed funds of $99,800,000 would come from the sale of bonds, eventually purchased by investors around the country.

The first step was to find the best chief engineer and designer who could make this project a reality. Three engineers were asked to interview and submit proposals. Rather fortuitously, the members of the Bridge Authority wound up with their third choice, David B. Steinman. Sixty-three years old, five feet tall, yet bigger than life, Steinman was a genius who received his engineering doctorate before the age of twenty. He had grown up admiring the wonders of the Brooklyn Bridge. In his younger years, as a newsboy, he told his buddies that some day he was going to build bridges like the famous structure that was towering above them. His friends just shook their heads and laughed at him. No one was laughing now at the man who had already built four hundred bridges and was about to reach the pinnacle of his career.

The devil was in the details, and Steinman presented them to the fullest. Along with his team of 350 engineers, Steinman meticulously mapped out more than 85,000 comprehensive blueprints. Worries about the rocks' strength underneath the Straits were put to rest by geologists who confirmed that the rocks had already passed their toughest trial. Over the past 1 million years, the rocks had been tested by a single, solid glacier, up to five miles high, that exerted ten to fifty times more pressure than would be placed on them by the bridge's foundations. There was no question that the rocks of Mackinac were sturdy enough to accept the million tons of concrete and steel that would become the anchors.

The bridge would be the world's largest suspension bridge, designed to accommodate dramatic changes in wind and temperature. The plans were approved, and crews were hired. The celebratory festivities began on May 7, 1954, and lasted two days, signaling the beginning of the construction that would bring the five-mile-long Mackinac Bridge to fruition.

More than 11,000 ironworkers, tradesmen, and volunteers toiled as a team, putting the pieces together, almost like an erector set. Barges were towed in, bringing in such things as 5 million rivets, 1 million bolts, and steel cables long enough to circle the equator twice. Three-quarters of the bridge would be sitting underwater, as a solid concrete foundation.

The physical labor was intense, and Michigan's northern weather forced the workers to endure everything nature could throw at them. In 1955 a storm blew over the Straits, the likes of which had not been seen in some fifteen years. Winds over 70 miles per hour blew towering waves crashing over the unfinished bridge, almost toppling the trestle. A second storm whirled in the next week, sinking a tug, but the bridge stood firm. Everyone was given a break during the blustery winters, when all work ceased, usually sometime in December.

In the peak of construction season, crews gave it their all, even at night, when they were stringing the cable. Steinman aesthetically described the scene to the Mackinac Bridge Authority: "Lights were strung along the catwalk . . . like a necklace of pearls and inspired artists and poets. . . . The beauty of the lines and forms as seen by day will be continued in poetry and magic at night."

The extreme altitudes that workers had to contend with were challenging. Five people lost their lives during construction. Two died their first day on the job when the catwalk collapsed. Two others lost their balance, falling into the Straits below. And a diver resurfaced too quickly from a depth of 140 feet, succumbing to decompression illness.

Finally, on November 1, 1957, after seventy years of haggling and only three-and-a-half years of construction, the majestic "Mighty Mac" was completed and ready to open, on schedule and within the budget. The Upper and Lower Peninsulas, through the tiny towns of St. Ignace and Mackinac City, would be eternally united. It was an engineering masterpiece that would forever change the way of life for Michigan. State Representative Clayton Morrison declared, as quoted in *Michigan History Magazine,* "The North and South of the state have long been engaged; they now have a wedding ring."

Steinman's summary of his creation to Lawrence Rubin, Executive Secretary for the Mackinac Bridge Authority was perhaps the best: "The Mackinac Bridge has been a challenge and an opportunity—a challenge to conquer the impossible, to build a bridge that people said couldn't be built. Aerodynamically it is the safest bridge in the world. It is a symphony in steel and stone that may well be called the bridge that faith has built."

MOTOR CITY GIVES
BIRTH TO MOTOWN

1959

An eight-year-old boy sat in the living room of his Detroit home, mesmerized by the reaction to the historic knockout victory on June 22, 1938, of boxing champ Joe Louis over Max Schmeling. All over the city, people were displaying ecstasy over the news, igniting a passion inside this observant and proud young African American. With wide eyes he asked himself, "How could I ever do anything in my life that could make this many people happy?" It wouldn't be too many years before his own cutting-edge ingenuity would turn the music world upset down, and Berry Gordy Jr. would have people everywhere "Dancing in the Streets."

The allure of the boxing ring was beating out his interest in scholastics, and at age sixteen, Gordy dropped out of school. He was slightly built—just five feet six inches tall and weighing 112 pounds—and his success as a fighter was limited, earning $150 for each of his ten victories.

He worked assorted stints: a soldier in the Korean War, a failed record-store owner, and an assembly-line worker at Lincoln-Mercury.

By age twenty-nine, he was a divorced father of three, living with sister, and virtually broke. Throughout it all, in the back of his mind, there was always the throbbing rhythm of music.

Armed with an $800 loan from his family, he ventured out as a songwriter, scoring a hit with "Reet Petite," which he cowrote with boxer-singer Jackie Wilson. His next song, the Miracles' "Got a Job," brought in a paltry royalty check of $3.19. The melodies were there. The money wasn't.

A gambler at heart, Gordy took a risk in opening his own record-ing studio in a small house on West Grand Boulevard, which he called "Hitsville USA," since that was the only name he could think of that fully expressed the type of business he envisioned it to be: a hip factory building hit after hit. On December 14, 1959, Motown Records, the first music company in the United States owned by an African American, was officially given life inside the humble two-story building.

The music he felt flowing through his veins was different from anything he'd ever heard. The black community already had its rhythm and blues. This new sound would shatter racial barriers, bringing blacks and whites together to hum the same tunes for the first time. A rhythmic bebop jazz would be one way to describe it. Deviating from tradition, all the lyrics would be in the present tense.

Gordy made a conscious decision to have exclusively black artists who symbolized the struggles of their race. Motown would be "Afro-American music, without apology." Looking at his own life and the experiences of his fellow African Americans, Gordy soon recognized one of the biggest challenges they all shared: money, or lack thereof. One of the first songs recorded in his new studio was the prophetic "Money (That's What I Want)," on the Tamla label, #54027. Gordy purposely assigned it a large number so people wouldn't know how young his label was, he explained. (Originally he wanted to call it Tammy, after Debbie Reynolds's blockbuster hit of the same name, but that was already taken.)

The vision for his fledgling company was clear-cut, thanks, in part, to his days on the assembly line. Mass-producing hit records efficiently was his main objective, and Gordy made a fundamental comparison between the auto industry and his record company in his autobiography, *To Be Loved,* when he said, "At the plant cars started out as just a frame . . . until they emerged at the end of the line—brand spanking new cars rolling off the line. I wanted the same concept for my company, only with artists and songs and records. I wanted a place where a kid off the street could walk in one door an unknown and come out another a recording artist—a star."

Duplicating the automotive process, Gordy had departments of quality control (to make sure the sound was just right), product evaluation (where groups would assess a record's potential to become a hit), and tour support (a "charm school" where the artists would be groomed for mainstream perfection with clothing and manners).

Gordy had a knack for hiring the best talent available, both on and off stage. The studio needed to produce a master sound on a shoestring budget, so the downstairs bathroom became the first echo chamber. An employee was assigned to guard the door to make sure no one flushed a toilet during a recording session.

Sound effects stretched imaginations. Gordy admitted that the studio would do anything to create a unique percussion sound. Sometimes they would slap two blocks of wood together or hit small mallets on glass astrays. They even went so far as to have the rhythm section shake jars of dried peas. Their creativity would stop at nothing. Union musicians made concessions to help out. Instead of working three hours for $60, they came in at odd times, willing to work for as little as $5.

The hits began to stream out of Studio A, which musicians referred to as "The Snakepit." It was unbelievably cramped, with an amplifying wood floor and isolation booth for the singers built into the wall. The studio ran twenty-two hours a day, shutting down between 8:00 and 10:00 a.m. for maintenance. The public had no idea, nor did they care where the sound was produced, embracing it wholeheartedly.

It really was all about the sound, and Gordy knew that better than anyone. He listened to the music just as the audience would. The majority of young people were listening to his popular songs on their car radios. To fine-tune the radio sound, he had his head engineer, Mike McLean, build a simulated car radio in the studio. Berry's attention to detail delighted his audience—and record sales reflected that.

According to *Billboard,* the bible of the music industry, Motown, during its first ten years, chalked up eight Top 10 records. Before 1988 it had more than one hundred number-one hits. The stars Motown created were a *Who's Who* of music, including Diana Ross and the Supremes (with an unprecedented record of five consecutive number-one songs), Marvin Gaye, the Jackson Five, the Temptations, the Four Tops, and Stevie Wonder.

Detroit's "civil disturbance" of 1967 put a permanent damper on the spirit of Motown Records, which announced in June 1972 that it was moving to Los Angeles. The company was sold to a group of private investors for $61 million in 1988, at which time Gordy proudly announced that he had taken an eight hundred dollar investment and turned it into sixty-one million. No one could argue that his gamble had paid off, winning him the ultimate poker hand.

WORLD SERIES HEALS WOUNDS

1968

In 1968 the country needed a major Band-Aid, probably more so in Detroit than anyplace else. The prior year had been a difficult one. Riots in the summer of 1967 had marked the resurgence of racial tensions, and the city was bitterly disappointed when the Detroit Tigers lost the pennant in the final play of the season's final game.

Baseball offered hope in a city that clearly had been wounded. Yet this year, too, was already marred with tragedy. The funeral of Martin Luther King in April 1968 delayed opening day. The Vietnam War weighed heavily on everyone's mind amid reports that more guns had been purchased in Detroit than at any other time in the city's history.

By the time Earl Wilson threw out the first pitch on April 10, 1968, there had been a lot of suffering. And that day wasn't good either, as the Tigers lost 7–3.

But the winds of change were about to blow across Tiger Stadium as the team broke out on a major winning streak. By April 29 they had won nine consecutive games. On May 10 they jumped to first place and never let go.

Some incredible things were happening at the ball park on the corner of Michigan and Trumbull in a season that has come to be known as "the year of the pitcher." Twenty-four-year-old Denny McLain became a meteoric sensation, going 31–6 for the season, the first pitcher to win thirty games since Dizzy Dean back in 1934. His (likely never to be matched) thirty-first record-setting victory on September 14 was overshadowed when Mickey Mantle hit his 535th career home run; Mantle vowed that McLain had planned to let him hit it out of the park.

The come-from-behind team was making a comeback. Thirty of their victories were clinched by the game's last batter. Most others were won after the seventh inning. The Tigers' bats were swinging so powerfully that they topped the league with 185 home runs and 671 runs scored. Jim Northrup hit two grand slams in one game on June 24. That same day, shortstop Don Wert was hit by a pitch so strong that it smashed his helmet, hospitalizing him for a couple of days.

For two months the team was without the help of its leading hitter, Al Kaline, who in late May had been hit by a wild pitch, breaking his arm. Defiantly, catcher Bill Freehan, hoping to demonstrate his resiliency, allowed himself to be hit by a pitch twenty-four times.

The season was on its way to pumping up a deeply deflated city. On September 17 the team officially won the American League pennant in front of 46,512 hometown fans, paving the way to the long-awaited World Series, for the first time since 1945.

Fighting them for the championship would be the National League's pennant-winning St. Louis Cardinals, featuring their superstar pitcher, Bob Gibson, who was 22–9 for the season, with a record-setting earned-run average of 1.12.

The fearless Tigers weren't threatened when they took the mound in St. Louis for game one of the series on October 2. Their ace Denny McLain was confidently ready to battle Gibson. Manager

Mayo Smith did face a tough decision concerning Al Kaline, who had been out for thirty-seven games. Should Smith put Kaline in the lineup at his usual right field position? He decided to do so, moving Mickey Stanley to shortstop for the first time in his career.

Before long, it became obvious that Gibson was at the top of his game, striking out seventeen batters for a shutout, 4–0. McLain was taken out in the sixth inning.

The next afternoon, Mickey Lolich took the mound for the Tigers. A solid left-handed pitcher going 17–9 for the season and somewhat out of shape, he surprised everyone by hitting a home run, the first and only of his sixteen-year career. He racked up the victory for game two with a score of 8–1.

The Tigers then came back home to Detroit, where they hoped to move ahead in game three. That wasn't to be. Even though the Tigers hit two home runs, the Cardinals' batting power fared better, winning 7–3.

Game four was a rematch between McLain and Gibson. After giving up six runs in the first three innings, McLain was sent back to the dugout. Two rain delays over an hour long left a glimmer of hope. Manager Smith tried stalling, hoping that the game would be called early. The Cardinals' manager countered by trying to hurry things up. In the end, it was an embarrassment for the Tigers, who lost 10–1. Sportswrters across the country concurred that they had never seen any team play so poorly in the World Series.,

Down three games to one, the Tigers were facing a do-or-die game five in Detroit, where, in an ironic twist, musical history was made. The Tigers' announcer, Ernie Harwell, had invited Jose Feliciano to sing the national anthem. Never having sung it publicly before, Feliciano gave it his own interpretation, a unique, slow, soulful rendition, which was greeted with boos from local fans. Mickey Lolich, who was initially irritated by the long, drawn-out rendition, regained his composure and pitched the entire game, earning the much-needed win, 5–3.

Game six found McLain back in action on only two days of rest. The Tigers' bats were hot, scoring ten runs in the third inning, including a grand slam by Northrup. McLain's steady arm gave him his win, 13–1.

The moment of truth had arrived—game seven! Oddsmakers favored the Cardinals, who were playing on their home turf. With the series tied at 3–3, hearts in Detroit were beating rapidly.

Again, on only two days of rest, Lolich was back, to face his pitching duel with the dreaded Gibson. In the locker room, Smith encouraged his players, telling them that Gibson was not Superman, to which wise-cracking Tiger first baseman Norm Cash responded that he had just seen him in a telephone booth changing his clothes.

Inning after inning, each pitcher held his ground, keeping the other team scoreless until the seventh inning, when Gibson granted singles to Norm Cash and Willie Horton, followed by Northrup's triple.

By the end of the game, the Tigers beat the Cardinals 4–1, setting off a rash of raucous joy. Lolich jumped into Freehan's arms for the classic photo, later exclaiming, "If I didn't leap into his arms, he would have jumped on me first."

When the team arrived back in Motor City, 35,000 fans showed up to congratulate them at Metro Airport—so many, in fact, that it was unsafe to land, causing the plane to be diverted to Willow Run instead.

Mickey Lolich had won three World Series games, a feat never to be repeated, earning him the MVP award, while Denny McLain claimed the prestigious Cy Young award.

The year 1968 was the last time there were no post-season play-offs, and may have been the last time to really claim a "hometown" team. At least four of the '68 Tigers were native Michiganders: Bill Freehan, from Royal Oak; Jim Northrup, from Breckenridge, a small town west of Saginaw; Mickey Stanley, from Grand Rapids; and Detroit's own Willie Horton, who once had youthful aspirations of being a boxer.

The Tigers' World Series victory did more than give Detroit a winning baseball team; it unified a city on the mend. Team owner John Fetzer told the team how proud he was of them for not only winning the pennant and the series, but also for saving the city.

But it was Willie Horton who spoke the immortal words that stand today in the new Comerica Park: "I believe the '68 Tigers were put here by God to heal this city."

ARTHUR HILL PLAYS
TO PERFECTION

1973

Every athlete aspires to be on that once-in-a-lifetime dream team. In 1973 the members of Saginaw's Arthur Hill High School football team saw their greatest wish come true.

That year they won the big one, the equivalent of the Super Bowl, but with a Triple Crown bonus. Back then there was no official state championship game as there is today. Instead, the media sportswriters declared which team was the best, and there was no disputing that the fighting Lumberjacks were on top of their game. They had gone 9–0 for the season, and received four Class A championship trophies from the United Press International, Associated Press, *Detroit News,* and *Detroit Free Press.*

It wasn't just their win/loss record that gave them first-class status; it was *how* they achieved that record. That year, not only were the Lumberjacks undefeated, none of their opponents were able to score even a single point against them, while they racked up some monster scores. The final tally: Lumberjacks: 443; opponents: 0.

This averaged out to 49.2 points per game, or more than one point a minute.

As incredible as it may seem, nineteen teams in Michigan have accomplished the same feat. Yet very few of them (and none in recent memory) were in Class A. The last time a Class A team went undefeated and unscored upon was in 1933. The Charlevoix Rayders pulled off similar victories in 1945, going 6–0, and again in 1958, when they earned the Northern Michigan Class C championship with a record of 8–0, scoring "only" 321 points.

As time goes by, the distinction becomes even more exceptional. No team in the state has managed to keep all its opponents scoreless since Arthur Hill did so.

It wasn't always that way for them, though. They were winless in both 1968 and 1969, and their combined record for the three years including 1970 was 1–25–1. The team was in desperate need of a turnaround.

Enter George Ihler, a twenty-seven-year-old former football player from Western Michigan University, who became coach in 1971. In sports, physical strength is only part of the equation. The other part could be called the brain game. And that's where Ihler was a master. He was aggressive, passionate, and more determined than ever to win a major title.

Along with a young and energetic group of assistants, he pounded the players with positive thoughts. He also pounded them on the field, tackling them during practices. Ilher and his coaching staff would get right in there with the team, allowing the players to see all of them as real people, taking hits as hard as as anyone else, and setting the stage for a competitive thirst. By the end of Ihler's first season, the team finished with a respectable 4–4–1. The next year, with a team of mostly juniors, they jumped to an astounding 8–1. The comeback kids were on their way.

At the beginning of the 1973 season, the Lumberjacks, now stacked with seniors, had a clearly defined objective: to win the state championship. Ihler worked the media hard, and after his team's first 40–0 victory against Midland, the Associated Press gave the top ranking in the state to Arthur Hill. His strategy was to get the players in the top slot right from the beginning, making it easier for them to stay focused on remaining there.

The plan worked. Game two (51–0), game three (55–0), game four (46–0), game five (40–0), and game six (66–0) were easy victories. Credit goes in part to the tough engine of the offense. Rarely did they need to pass; rushing was more their style, which made perfect sense. The Lumberjacks' beefy front-line blockers averaged 220 pounds each, and they were speedy. The *Saginaw News* wrote that the quickness of the line was "like grease from a frying pan."

Electricity was in the air for game seven, an away game against the Flint Northern Vikings, ranked number five in the Associated Press poll. In the bleachers sat 10,000 of the Vikings' fans, their mouths agape, awed by what they saw. The score rapidly jumped to 14–0 even before their team ever had control of the ball. When it was over, Arthur Hill had trounced the Vikings, with a score of 34–0.

The perfect season with the accompanying championship was just one game away. The Lumberjacks' confidence was riding high, yet they were aware this would be the ultimate test against their biggest rivals, the Saginaw High Trojans. On November 2, less than ideal conditions prevailed—cold, wind, and, by the end of the game, blowing snow.

Leading at half-time 50–0, the Lumberjacks were the favorites to win the game. But could they hold their opponents scoreless? Coach Ihler remained fearless to the point of putting in the second string. With just seconds left in the game, Saginaw's kickoff return carried the ball past one tackler, then another, as everyone held their breath.

The third tackler was the charm, ending the phenomenal season with a 64–0 victory.

Afterward, the scene in the locker room was more exhilarating than New Year's Eve and the Fourth of July put together. The players of Arthur Hill had accomplished what previously had been unimaginable.

Their statistics were astounding. During the entire season, the first-string team scored forty-eight out of the fifty-four times they controlled the ball and committed only three turnovers on one fumble and two interceptions.

On top of the championship titles, the three co-captains— center Terry Murphy, quarterback Ron Rummel, and halfback Terry Eurick—along with offensive lineman Paul Walderzak earned first-team all-state honors. Thirteen other players earned all-league honors.

Eurick went on to play football at Notre Dame, gracing the cover of *Sports Illustrated* on January 9, 1978, with a dynamic photo and the headline "Terry Eurick Shocks Texas." He scored two touchdowns in the Cotton Bowl, upsetting the Texas Longhorns 38–10, and earned most of the credit for Notre Dame's national championship.

Years later, Eurick said that his Notre Dame victories may have been bigger than his championship title with Arthur Hill but doubted they were ever better.

As for Coach Ihler, he remained with the Lumberjacks until 1983 and then coached eleven years at Saginaw Valley State, where his record was 61–52–1. Although he was always successful, the highlight of his career will forever be the unsurpassed season of Saginaw's Arthur Hill High Lumberjacks, who are still deemed to be the best high school football team Michigan has ever had.

INDOOR GRASS SETS
NEW SOCCER STANDARD

1994

The World Cup is the international equivalent of the Super Bowl. Both are dedicated to recognizing the best in football—except in the United States, where World Cup football has always been called soccer. In 1930 Montevideo, Uruguay, was the site of the very first tournament, which attracted a scant thirteen teams. Since then, the World Cup has soared in popularity, attracting an elite, if not snobbish, following. When it was announced that the Silverdome in Pontiac, Michigan, would host the 1994 World Cup, reactions were anything but favorable. How could the sport be played indoors when it was required that the field be natural grass? The state was determined to prove all these doubts meritless.

Headquartered in Zurich, Switzerland, FIFA (Fédération Internationale de Football Association)—the second-largest international organization in the world, after the United Nations—took a lot of heat for granting such a prestigious event to such an unlikely candidate. FIFA's decision was considered extremely radical; never in its history had the World Cup—the pièce de résistance of soccer—been played indoors. In the summer, baseball was being played in most of the outdoor stadiums in the United States, leaving few remaining choices. The irony may have been that for the first time, European football would be played in an American football stadium, without the artificial turf.

The turf at the Silverdome would receive neither rain nor sunshine, so local organizers had to find a green-thumb wizard who could get grass to grow indoors in the absence of natural light. They sought out the very best agriculture specialists and found them in their own backyard, at Michigan State University (MSU) in East Lansing.

For the organizers, the high stakes were clearly spelled out. A successful event would infuse more than $120 million into the local economy and leave a favorable impression of their accomplishments in the eyes of the world. Should the efforts fail, Michigan may have been permanently removed from the soccer map.

From the university's Department of Crop and Social Sciences, members of the sod squad were assembled: John N. Rogers II, John Stier, James R. Crum, and Paul E. Rieke. The team of turfgrass scientists recognized that this would be an experimental exercise. Top-quality indoor grass was questionable at best. How do you grow lavish, rich grass inside a cave? With a high level of risk and a two-year window, time was not on their side.

Access to the Silverdome was limited because the Detroit Lions regularly practiced and played there. To compensate, the scientists constructed an exact replica in August 1992 at the MSU Hancock Turfgrass Research Center. This mock research dome differed only in size, filling just 6,600 square feet, compared to 77,625 square feet for a full-size international soccer field.

The "Silverdome West" was set up precisely as its counterpart and covered with the same fabric, which eliminates 90 percent of natural sunlight and most of the blue light necessary to the growth of plant life. Test after test was conducted in search of the perfect final product.

Many hands got dirty digging in the dirt, and the scientists worked with multiple combinations of seeds and soil. To determine which combination was the best, they needed to conduct real-life test trials. The sod squad cried, "Bring the players," and the MSU soccer team stormed in, pounding the turf with a series of dribbles, passes, and kicks. This may have been the first time in history that athletes were asked to practice not to test their skills, but rather to test the effectiveness of a blade of grass.

After the turf endured numerous bouncing balls and banana kicks, the scientists put their faith in a mixture of 85 percent Kentucky bluegrass and 15 percent perennial ryegrass. During the winter, acres and acres of the blend started their life in California, growing quietly while waiting to be shipped cross-country to Michigan in temperature-controlled refrigerated trucks.

On March 1, 1993, more than a year in advance of the first game, construction crews began assembling the field, laboring ten to twelve hours every day until April 22, when it was time to place the crowning glory. Having survived a safe return from the West, the sod now sat in a parking lot shed. Needing every bit as much care as a newborn baby, the grass had to be watered and mowed every day, with scheduled fertilizing.

Everything was in place, all systems were go, and it was time for the sod's first real full-time game. The first major sporting event ever to be played on natural grass in the Silverdome took place on June 19, 1993. On that day, the "experiment" was put to the test with the finals of the U.S. Cup, when Germany beat England in front of an audience of 62,000 people. Participants hailed the grass as "perfect," and FIFA officials who were observing praised it as a "huge success."

The grass had proved its mettle as being World Cup–worthy. Now, as ridiculous as it may sound, the entire field had to be painstakingly taken apart, stored, and then reassembled the following year. All the while, the high-maintenance grass required almost round-the-clock doses of nurturing.

It was this constant skilled "nursing" of the grass that fascinated the international media. News outlets from as far away as Japan, Switzerland, Great Britain, and Mexico broadcast scenes of the lawn being mowed to their television viewers back home. Television cameras followed fertilizer personnel throughout the day.

The experimental stage was over, and now it was showtime. On Saturday, June 18, 1994, a horribly hot and humid day, more than 70,000 fans sweated in a jammed stadium without any air-conditioning and watched the United States and Switzerland play to a 1–1 tie in the first World Cup soccer game ever to have been played indoors.

Competition continued through June 28. Throughout the numerous games, the grass performed flawlessly, except for needing an occasional divot repair. Not a single complaint was uttered about the nearly $2 million sod. The sod squad had been victorious. New attendance records for the games were set, while the world's opinion of Michigan and its agricultural prowess rose to new heights. The state had accomplished what most people thought was an impossible feat.

After the games, nine new putting greens somewhere became the beneficiary of the technically advanced soil. And the sod was transferred to Detroit's Belle Isle so that local residents could kick back on what was likely the world's most expensive turf.

MICHIGAN FACTS AND TRIVIA

- Michigan officially became the twenty-sixth state in the Union on January 26, 1837, after giving up rights to Toledo in exchange for the Upper Peninsula.

- The state's official nickname is the Great Lakes State, although since the 1830s people have often referred to it as the Wolverine State. No one can remember the last time they saw a wolverine outside of a zoo—that is, until February 2004, when a single male was spotted in Ubley, near the top of Michigan's thumb.

- It seems that almost everything has an official designation. The brook trout became the state fish in 1988; the robin is the state bird (1931); the white pine is the state tree (1955); the Isle Royale greenstone is the state gem (1973); Petoskey stone is the state stone (1965); the painted turtle is the state reptile (1995); and Kalkaska dirt is the certified soil (1990).

- Michigan's motto is *Si quaeris peninsulam Amoenam Circumspice,* or "If you seek a pleasant peninsula, look about you."

- The Hopewell Indians, who arrived in Michigan in 10 BC, built burial mounds until AD 400, when for some unknown reason they discontinued the practice. It's believed that descendants of the Hopewells still live in Michigan today. The best-preserved Hopewellian burial center in the country is the Norton Mound Group in Grand Rapids.

- In 1777 the British began conducting raids from Detroit into Kentucky, capturing a well-known Kentuckian, Daniel Boone, and bringing him back to Detroit as a prisoner.

- The territory of Michigan was established in 1805, with Detroit as its first capital. That same year, the city was completely destroyed by fire.

- In the early 1800s, the residents of Monroe began their more than two-hundred-year-old tradition of eating muskrat for their winter meals.

- Public stagecoaches made their debut in 1822.

- Michigan has 116 lighthouses. The oldest was built in 1825 at Fort Gratiot. Its replacement, constructed in 1828, still stands.

- In 1846 Michigan became the first state to abolish the death penalty for all crimes except treason.

- Construction of the Soo locks began in 1853, taking two years to complete. Representing the largest waterway traffic system anywhere on earth, the locks allow ships to adjust to the twenty-one-foot difference between Lake Superior and the Lower Great Lakes.

- On July 6, 1854, the Republican Party was born, "Under the Oaks" in Jackson.

- Fred Sanders opened his first candy shop in downtown Detroit on June 17, 1875, satisfying taste buds with his sumptuous hot-fudge dessert topping. His inimitable recipe remains top secret to this day.

- The first patent for a carpet sweeper was awarded in 1876 to Melville Bissell of Grand Rapids. He invented the sweeper after he had grown tired of listening to his wife, Anna, complain about how difficult it was to pick up sawdust on the carpeting inside their crockery shop.

- Since 1883 East Jordan Iron Works (the unofficial sewer capital of the world) has been manufacturing street castings for almost every city you've ever set foot in.

- In 1886 the BB gun was invented in Plymouth, earning it the distinction of "BB Gun Capital of the World."

- It took less than four months to construct Mackinac Island's famous Grand Hotel, which opened in 1887. It boasts the world's largest columned porch, at 660 feet in length. Five hundred thousand gallons of water are required to fill the serpentine-shaped swimming pool, built for Esther Williams's movie *This Time for Keeps* (1947).

- An 1884 accident in the kitchen of Battle Creek's Seventh Day Adventist health facility created a new industry. The Kellogg brothers decided to bake some stale leftover wheat, inventing the first cornflake cereal.

- Charles Brady King drove the first "horseless carriage," aka the gasoline-powered automobile, down the streets of Detroit on March 6, 1896. It wasn't until three months later that Henry Ford drove his first vehicle.

- The year 1903 marks the first time the Scottville Clown Band began tooting their own horns. Now, with more than two hundred members, they still march to the beat of their own drummer, wearing hula skirts and outrageous costumes, all while playing some top-quality music.

- Competition within the auto industry began in 1903. In that year, William C. Durant organized General Motors, while Henry Ford introduced the coveted Model T.

- In 1919 newlyweds Harry and Bess Truman spent their honeymoon at the Harrington Inn in Port Huron. Their daughter, Margaret, later wrote in the biography of her mother, entitled *Bess W. Truman,* "For the rest of his life, whenever Harry Truman wanted to regain the radiance of those first days with Bess, he simply wrote, 'Port Huron.' For him it was a code word for happiness."

- Detroit's Cadieux Café brought the Belgian tradition of feather bowling to the city's east side in 1929. Fans of the sport continue to throw a three-and-a-quarter-pound wooden disc down a seventy-foot concave trough covered with dirt and ox blood.

- In 1930 Mabel White Holmes whipped up her first batch of Jiffy Mix in Chelsea. The company continues to produce 950,000 boxes of twenty-two varieties every day. Everything, right down to the cute little box, is still made at that very same location.

- Simplicity Patterns began manufacturing their famous patterns for creative sewers in Niles in 1931. The company closed its doors here in September 2007.

- This fact may not make Michigan State fans happy who have always thought of themselves as the first Spartans. The Detroit Lions were originally the Spartans, purchased out of Portsmouth, Ohio, on June 30, 1934, for a value-priced

$7,952.08. The new owners quickly changed the name of the team to pair with the already jungle-themed Detroit Tigers. In 2008 the Lions became the first team in NFL history to lose all sixteen of their regular season games.

- The oldest Santa Claus School in the world is housed in Midland, currently under the direction of Tom and Holly Valent. The first class to teach Santa and Mrs. Claus how to share the love and laughter of the season was held in 1937.

- Frankenmuth is home to the world's largest Christmas store, Bronner's CHRISTmas Wonderland. Since 1945 it's grown to a whopping seven and a quarter acres, the equivalent of five and a half football fields.

- In 1947 in Cassopolis, Ed Lowe invented Kitty Litter, growing it into a business with $200 million in annual sales.

- Brothers Peter and Jerry Cusimano started the tradition of throwing an octopus at Detroit Red Wings games. The fish market owners flung the premier eight-legged cephalopod across the ice at Olympia Stadium on April 15, 1952.

- The Pistons basketball team, originally from Fort Wayne, Indiana, became the Detroit Pistons in 1957. For thirty-two years they tried to win an NBA championship, but it wasn't until they left the Silverdome far behind them, to relocate to the much-luckier Palace of Auburn Hills, that they won their back-to-back championships in 1989 and 1990.

- On Saturday, June 17, 1967, the Detroit Tigers played the longest double-header in American League history, lasting a total of nine hours and five minutes. The Tigers won the first game in nine innings, beating Kansas City 7–6. The second game carried on for nineteen innings. This time the Tigers weren't so lucky, losing by a heartbreaking score of 6–5.

- The popular pinch-hitter for the 1968 Detroit Tigers, Gates Brown, with a .370 batting average, was signed by the team while serving prison time in Ohio.

- Michigan's own Gerald Rudolph Ford Jr., formerly known as Leslie Lynch King Jr., was the only person to ever become both vice president and president without ever receiving a single vote. On December 3, 1973, he replaced Vice President Spiro Agnew, who resigned over tax evasion issues. On August 9, 1974, Ford became president, replacing Richard Nixon, who left the White House because of the Watergate scandal.

- Finally, isn't it comforting to know that every time Americans say the Pledge of Allegiance, they're really putting a map of Michigan across their heart?

BIBLIOGRAPHY

Pageant of the Sault—1671

About Statistics Canada: Jean Talon, www.statcan.gc.ca /about-apercu/jt/eng.htm.

Bayliss, Joseph E., and Estelle L. Bayliss. *River of Destiny*. Detroit: Wayne University Press, 1955.

Kellogg, Louise P., ed. *Early Narratives of the Northwest*. New York: Charles Scribner's Sons, 1917.

Sault Ste. Marie History, www.saultstemarie.org/index .php?option=com_content&view=.

Wisconsin Historical Society. "American Journeys Collection: The Pageant of 1671," Document #AJ-050, Digital Libraries & Archives, 2003.

The *Griffon* Sets Sail—1679

Boyer, Dwight. *Great Stories of the Great Lakes*. Cornwall, NY: Cornwall Press, 1966.

Donahue, James. "LaSalle's Griffin, First Great Lakes Ship," http: //perdurabo10.tripod.com/ships/id103.html.

Ellis, William Donahue. *Land of the Inland Seas*. Palo Alto, CA: American West Publishing, 1974.

Hancock, Paul. *Shipwrecks of the Great Lakes*. Holt, MI: Thunder Bay Press, 2001.

Kohl, Chris. *Shipwreck Tales of the Great Lakes*. West Chicago, IL: Seawolf Communications, 2004.

"The Griffin," Absolute Michigan, www.absolutemichigan.com /dig/michigan/the-griffin/.

Chief Pontiac's Siege on Fort Detroit—1763

Dowd, Gregory Evans. *War under Heaven: Pontiac, the Indian Nations, and the British Empire.* Baltimore: Johns Hopkins University Press, 2002.

Kallen, Stuart A. *Native American Chiefs and Warriors.* San Diego: Lucent Books, 1999.

Nolan, Jenny. "Chief Pontiac's Siege of Detroit," *Detroit News,* June 14, 2000.

Peckham, Howard H. *Pontiac and the Indian Uprising.* New York: Russell and Russell, 1947.

Battle of the River Raisin—1813

Bak, Rickard. "River Raisin's Bloody Banks," *Hour Magazine,* June 2009.

Rosentreter, Roger L. "Battle of the River Raisin," *Michigan History Magazine,* January/February 2007.

"The Battle of Frenchtown," www.riverraisinbattlefield.org/the_ battles.htm.

"The Battle of the River Raisin," War of 1812 Digitization Project, The Monroe County Library System and the Monroe County Historical Commission, http://Monroe.lib.mi.us/war_of_1812 /raisin_river.htm.

"The River Raisin Massacre," www.monroeartleague.com/river_ raisin_massacre.htm.

Stomaching a Medical Discovery—1822

Burns, Virginia Law. *William Beaumont, Frontier Doctor.* Laingsburg, MI: Enterprise Press, 1978.

Edwards, Elizabeth. "The Gruesome Medical Breakthrough of Dr. William Beaumont on Mackinac Island," May 18, 2010, www .mynorth.com.

Horsman, Reginald. *Frontier Doctor: William Beaumont, America's First Great Medical Scientist.* Columbia: University of Missouri Press, 1996.

Lieser, Julia F. "The Man with the See-Through Stomach." *Child Life,* June 1, 2002.

"William Beaumont's Life and Work," 2006, www.james.com /beaumont/dr_life.htm.

Toledo War—1835

Faber, Don. *The Toledo War: The First Michigan-Ohio Rivalry.* Ann Arbor: University of Michigan Press, 2008.

"Stevens T. Mason," http://en.wikipedia.org/wiki/Stevens_T._ Mason.

Todorov, Karen. "The Toledo War," Michigan Department of Education, Office of School Improvement.

"Toledo War," www.globalsecurity.org/military/ops/toledo-war .htm.

Discovering Iron Ore—1844

Burt, John S. (direct descendant of William A. Burt). "Boys, Look Around and See What You Can Find," *Michigan History Magazine,* November/December 1994.

"Recorded in Stone—Voices on the Marquette Iron Range—
William Austin Burt," http://voices.nmu.edu/content.asp.

Stiffler, Donna L. "The Iron Riches of Michigan's Upper
Peninsula," Department of Natural Resources, www.michigan
.gov/dnr.

"William Austin Burt," *Transactions of the Michigan Academy of
Science, Arts, and Letters,* May/June 1980.

Kentucky Raids the Underground Railroad—1847

"Glossary of Underground Railroad Terms," Owen Sound's Black
History, www.osblackhistory.com.

History of Cass County, Michigan. Chicago: Waterman, Watkins,
1882.

Stecker, Naseem. "A Stop on the Long Road to Freedom,"
Michigan Bar Journal, July 2005.

Tobin, Jacqueline L., with Hettie Jones. *From Midnight to Dawn:
The Last Tracks of the Underground Railroad.* New York:
Doubleday Publishing, 2007.

Orphan Train's First Hopeful Stop—1854

Eicher, Al, and Dave Eicher. "The Little Wanderers," *Michigan
History Magazine,* January 1, 2003.

Laurent, J. R. "Dowagiac Celebrates Ties to Orphan Train
History," *South Bend Tribune,* September 1, 2004.

Littlefield, Holly. *Children of the Orphan Trains.* Minneapolis:
Carolrhoda Books, 2001.

O'Connor, Stephen. *Orphan Trains: The Story of Charles Loring
Brace and the Children He Saved and Failed.* New York:
Houghton Mifflin, 2001.

Vogt, Martha Nelson, and Christina Vogt. *Searching for Home: Three Families from the Orphan Trains.* Hillsboro, KS: Triumph Press, 1995.

Warren, Andrea. *Orphan Train Rider: One Boy's True Story.* New York: Houghton Mifflin, 1996.

Assassinating a "King"—1856

Launius, Roger D. *Joseph Smith III: Pragmatic Prophet.* Urbana and Chicago: University of Illinois Press, 1988.

Pepper, Terry. "James Jesse Strang, the King of Beaver Island," December 2, 2007, www.terrypepper.com/lights/closeups /strang/strang.htm.

Rosentreter, Roger L. "The Island Kingdom of James Strang," *Michigan History Magazine,* November 1, 2003.

Volgenau, Gerry. "Self-Proclaimed King of Beaver Island's Reign Was Short, but Violent," Knight Ridder/Tribune News Service, March 11, 2002.

Battle of Manton—1882

Battle of Manton, Michigan Historical Marker, US 131, Manton, erected 1970.

"Battle of Manton," http://en.wikipedia.org/wiki/Cadillac,_ Michigan.

"Battling for the County Seat," Absolute Michigan, www .absolutemichigan.com.

Manton Historical Museum, "Welcome to Manton," www .mantonmichigan.org.

Massie, Larry B. *On the Road to Michigan's Past.* Allegan Forest, MI: Priscilla Press, 1995.

Logging Out of a Jam—1883

"Brief History of Lumbering in Michigan," Michigan Educational Portal for Interactive Content, www.michiganepic.org /lumbering/LumberingBriefHistory.html.

"Grand Rapids History: Explore: The Grand River: Friend and Foe," www.historygrandrapids.org.

"Grand Rapids History: Learn More: The Great Log Jam of 1883," www.historygrandrapids.org/learn.php?id=26.

Lupo, Lee. "Grand Jam of 1883," *Muskegon Chronicle,* July 12, 2008.

White, Stewart Edward. *The Great Log Jam.* Frank Leslie Publishing House, 1901.

Thousands Vowing "I Do"—1907

Barnett, LeRoy. "A Popular Spot to Tie the Knot," *Michigan History Magazine,* January 1, 2007.

Lessenberry, Jack. "Essay: Love and Marriage," February 15, 2007, http://jackshow.blogs.com/jack/200702/essay_love_and_.html.

Long, Heather. "Marriage Laws—Michigan," http://marriage .families.com/blog/marriage-laws-michigan-amp-illinois.

Michigan History: St. Joseph Wedding Capital U.S.A., http: //www.absolutemichigan.com/dig/michigan/michigan-history-st-joseph-wedding-capital-usa/.

Personal interview with St. Joseph Librarian and Historian Alicia Allen.

Vargo, George. "Lake Excursion Boats Spark Fond Memories," *Herald-Palladium,* September 1, 1982.

Assistance from Chris Hartman, Berrien County Clerk's Office.

Furniture Strike of 1911—1911

Combs, Heath E. "Monument to Honor 1911 Furniture Strikers," *Furniture Today,* October 18, 2006.

Harms, Dr. Richard H. "A Brief Look at the History of Grand Rapids Area Furniture Manufacturers Association," www .fm4furniture.org/grafma/htm.

"History of the Great Grand Rapids Furniture Strike of 1911," Communications Workers of America, November 7, 2008, www.cwa4034.com/index.php?option=com_content&view=art.

Lydens, Z. Z., ed. *The Story of Grand Rapids.* Grand Rapids: Kregel Publications, 1967.

Ransom, Frank Edward. *The City Built on Wood: A History of the Furniture Industry in Grand Rapids, 1850–1950.* Ann Arbor: Edwards Brothers, 1955.

"Sex, Lies and Woodworkers," *Wood and Wood Products,* January 1, 1995.

Summer Spark Sets Towns Ablaze—1911

"Fire Loss in Michigan," *New York Times,* July 13, 1911.

Haines, Deb. "MIGen Web Project," http://cheyboygancountymi .org/history/tower.html.

"Oscoda, MI Area Fire, July 1911," GenDisasters, www3 .gendisasters.com/michigan/9784/oscoda-mi-area-fire-jul.

"The 1911 Oscoda Fire," http://sydaby.eget.net/swe/jp_oscoda .htm.

Italian Hall Catastrophe—1913

Garrett, Nicole, and Bob Garrett. "Copper Mining Strike of 1913," Archives of Michigan, Michigan Department of Natural Resources and Environment website, December 2006.

Killingbeck, Dale. "Remembering a Tragedy," *Grand Rapids Press,* December 28, 2003.

Lehto, Steve. *Death's Door: The Truth Behind Michigan's Largest Mass Murder.* Troy, MI: Momentum Books, 2006.

Rubyan-Ling, Saronne. "The Michigan Copper Strike of 1913," *History Today,* March 1998.

Assorted entries from the website: www.angelfire.com /mi2/1913/19136.html.

Storm of 1913—1913

Boyer, Dwight. *True Tales of the Great Lakes.* Cornwall, NY: Cornwall Press, 1971.

Deedler, William R. "Hell Hath No Fury like a Great Lakes Fall Storm . . . Great Lakes White Hurricane, November, 1913," National Weather Service Weather Forecast Office, Detroit/ Pontiac, www.crh.noaa.gov/dtx/stm_1013.php.

Detroit News, November 13, 1913, p. 1.

Gillett, Stephanie. "A Perfect Storm (Lake Huron, November, 1913)," *Michigan History Magazine,* November 1, 2005.

"Great Lakes Storm of 1913," http://en.wikipedia.org/wiki/Great_ Lakes_Storm_of_1913.

Ratigan, William. *Great Lakes Shipwrecks and Survivals.* Grand Rapids, MI: William B. Eerdmans, 1960.

Willis, Glen. "The Great Storm of 1913," http://www .pointeauxbarqueslighthouse.org/preserve/shipwrecks/1913.

Cleaners and Dyers War—1924

"Detroit's Prohibition Purple Gang," All Sands, www.allsands.com /History/People/prohibitiondetr_us_gn.htm.

FBI, Freedom of Information and Privacy Acts, File 62-HQ-29632, Subject: Purple Gang, November 27, 1933.

Gribben, Mark. "Cleaners and Dyers War," The Malefactor's Register, http://markgribben.com.

Jones, Thom L. "The Colour Purple: Detroit's Early Mob," Mob Corner, 2008, http://realdealmafia.com/purplegang.html.

Kavieff, Paul R. *The Purple Gang: Organized Crime in Detroit.* New York: Barricade Books, 2000.

The Ossian Sweet Trial—1925

Boyle, Kevin. Arc of Justice: A Saga of Race, Civil Rights, and Murder in the Jazz Age. New York: Henry Holt, 2004.

Vine, Phyllis. *One Man's Castle: Clarence Darrow in Defense of the American Dream.* New York: HarperCollins, 2004.

Zacharias, Patricia. "'I Have to Die a Man or Live a Coward'—the Saga of Dr. Ossian Sweet," *Detroit News,* February 12, 2001.

Dramatic Rescue at the Pabst Mine—1926

Cox, Bruce K. *Perfectly Safe: The Pabst Mine Disaster of 1926.* Wakefield, MI: Agogeebic Press, 2006.

Holmio, Armas K. E. *History of the Finns in Michigan.* Detroit: Wayne State University Press, 2001.

Kimball, Kendrick. "The Great Escape at Ironwood," *Detroit News,* September 30, 1926.

Liesch, Matthew. "The Majestic Hills of Ironwood," *Michigan History Magazine,* March 1, 2007.

"Pabst Mine Disaster," Wikipedia, http://en.wikipedia.org/wiki
/Pabst_Mine_Disaster.

Bath School Disaster—1927

Bernstein, Arnie. *Bath Massacre: American's First School Bombing.*
Ann Arbor: University of Michigan Press, 2009.

Clinton County Republican News, June 30, 1927.

Collins, Kelly. "Columbine Incident Recalls '27 Massacre," *USA
Today,* April 28, 1999.

Ellsworth, M. J. *Bath School Disaster.* Self-published, 1927.

Hoffman, Kathy Barks. "A Dark Day in 1927," Associated Press,
1999.

Michigan historical marker: Bath School Disaster, http:
//michmarkers.com/Pages/SO631.htm.

Pawlak, Debra. "Just Another Summer Day: The Bath School
Disaster," www.themediadrome.com.

Battle of the Overpass—1937

"Battle of the Overpass, May 26, 1937," The Henry Ford Museum,
www.hfmgv.org/exhibits/fmc/battle.asp.

Heitmann, John A. *The Automobile and American Life.* Jefferson,
NC: McFarland, 2009.

Holusha, John. "A Joining of Three Varied Old Warriors," *New
York Times,* July 28, 1995.

"Labor: Strikes of the Week," *Time,* June 7, 1937.

Marcus, Greil, and Sollors, Werner, eds. *A New Literary History of
America.* Cambridge, MA: Belknap Press of Harvard University
Press, 2009.

Detroit Race Riots—1943

Baulch, Vivian M., and Patricia Zacharias. "The 1943 Detroit Race Riots," *Detroit News,* February 11, 1999, www.detnews.com/michiganhistory.

Brown, Earl. "The Truth about the Detroit Riot," *Harper's Magazine,* November 1943.

"Deep Trouble," *Time,* June 28, 1943.

Jackman, Michael. "The Summer of '43," *Metro Times,* June 18, 2003.

"Riotous Race Hate," *Newsweek,* June 28, 1943, pp. 42–43.

Japanese Balloon Bombs—1945

Heaton, Dan. "Balloon Bombs over Michigan during World War II," June 11, 2009, associatedcontent.com.

National Museum of the United States Air Force, Fact Sheet.

Pawlak, Debra Anne. *Farmington and Farmington Hills.* Chicago: Arcadia Publishing, 2003.

Personal interview with Michael Unsworth, history bibliographer for Michigan State University libraries.

Unsworth, Michael E. "Vengeance, Balloon Attacks on Michigan," *Michigan History Magazine,* March/April 1987.

Lost in Space: NW Flight 2501—1950

Accident Investigation Report, Civil Aeronautics Board, SA-215, File No. 1-0081, released January 18, 1951.

Heppenheimer, T. A. *Turbulent Skies: The History of Commercial Aviation.* New York: John Wiley & Sons, 1995.

Michigan Shipwreck Research Associates. "The Loss of Northwest Airlines Flight 2501—DC-4," www.michiganshipwrecks.org /dc4.htm.

"Northwest Flight 2501: Flight Plan, Witnesses, Victims," http: //NorthwestFlight2501.org.

"Northwest Orient Airlines Flight 2501," Wikipedia, http: //en.wikipedia.org/wiki/Northwest_Orient_Airlines_ Flight_2501.

Prichard, James. "1950 Airliner Crash Still a Mystery," *South Bend Tribune,* April 1, 2007.

Bridging the Gap—1957

Fornes, Mike. *Images of America, Mackinac Bridge.* Mount Pleasant, Arcadia Publishing, 2007.

"The History of the Bridge," Michigan Department of Transportation, www.mackinacbridge.org.

Rubin, Lawrence A. *The Official Picture History of the Mackinac Bridge.* Detroit: Wayne State University Press, 1958.

Zacharias, Pat. "The Breathtaking Mackinac Bridge," *Detroit News,* June 6, 2000, detnews.com/MichiganHistory.

Motor City Gives Birth to Motown—1959

About.com, Oldies Music, Profile: Motown, http://oldies.about .com/od/soulmotown/p/motown.htm.

Dennis, Robert. "Our Motown Heritage, Recording Snowshoes & Shovels," www.recordingequ.com/2006motown/06motown04 .html.

Gordy, Berry. *To Be Loved: The Music, the Magic, the Memories of Motown: An Autobiography.* New York: Warner Books, 1994.

Posner, Gerald. *Motown: Music, Money, Sex and Power*. New York: Random House, 2002.

Smith, Suzanne E. *Dancing in the Street: Motown and the Cultural Politics of Detroit*. Cambridge, MA: Harvard University Press, 1999.

World Series Heals Wounds—1968

Allen, Kevin M. *The People's Champion: Willie Horton*. Wayne, MI: Immortal Investments Publishing, 2004.

Cantor, George. *The Tigers of '68: Baseball's Last Real Champions*. Dallas: Taylor Publishing, 1997.

Falls, Joe. *The Detroit Tigers: An Illustrated History*. New York: Walker, 1989.

Harrigan, Patrick. *The Detroit Tigers: Club and Community, 1945–1995*. Toronto: University of Toronto Press, 1997.

Poremba, David Lee. *Baseball in Detroit, 1886–1968*. Charleston, SC: Arcadia Publishing, 1998.

Smith, Fred T. "Fifty Years with the Tigers," published by Fred T. Smith, Russ Entwistle, and John Duffy, Lathrup Village, Michigan, 1983.

Arthur Hill Plays to Perfection—1973

"Charlevoix Celebrates Legendary '58 Football Team," Petoskey News.com, October 14, 2008.

Saginaw County Sports Hall of Fame Inaugural Class, http://www.review-mag.com.

Schulz, Todd. "The Perfect Season," *Michigan History Magazine*, September/October 2007.

Sports Illustrated, volume 48, issue 2, January 9, 1978.

Indoor Grass Sets New Soccer Standard—1994

"1994 World Cup Schedule Includes First Indoor Match," *Boston Globe,* October 21, 1992.

Bondy, Filip. "Soccer: To Practice for 1994, a U.S. Cup Next June," *New York Times,* November 27, 1992.

Davis, Steve. "U.S. World Cup History 1930–2006," http.si.com.

Rogers, John N., III. "Indoor Turf/World Cup '94 Project Update," http://archive.lib.msu.edu/tic/mitgc./article/1995227 .pdf.

Vecsey, George. "Sports of the Times; Can Soccer Grow Grass under Foot?" *New York Times,* March 24, 1992.

Michigan Facts and Trivia

Absolute Michigan website, www.absolutemichigan.com.

Burcar, Colleen. *Michigan Curiosities,* second edition. Guilford, CT: Globe Pequot Press, 2007.

Burcar, Colleen. *You Know You're in Michigan When. . . .* Guilford, CT: Globe Pequot Press, 2005.

Port Huron Sesquicentennial Timeline, www.thetimesherald.com /article/20081024/NEWS/71005034.

INDEX

ABOUT THE AUTHOR

Colleen Burcar has worked as a reporter and news anchor in radio, television, and newspapers for many years in the Detroit area. She now works in media consulting and public relations, while her voice continues to be heard in numerous commercials. She is the author of *Michigan Curiosities* and *You Know You're in Michigan When . . .* and shares her love of Michigan in speaking engagements across the state. The mother of a daughter, Kimberly, Colleen currently resides in Bloomfield Hills with her husband, Bryan Becker, and toy poodle, Chloe.